A Million Pieces

FORGIVING AND HEALING AFTER BETRAYAL AND TRAUMA

THERESA MARIE

A MILLION PIECES:
FORGIVING AND HEALING AFTER BETRAYAL AND TRAUMA
by Theresa Marie

ISBNs: 978-1-953625-21-2 Trade Paperback | 978-1-953625-22-9 Ebook

Intelligent Design Press
An imprint of Kelley Creative
Spokane, Washington, USA

A Million Pieces

Forgiving and Healing After Betrayal and Trauma

Theresa Marie

Foreword

I AM GRATEFUL TO REV. THERESA for the masterful writing of this book and for sharing the ugly, horrible, embarrassing things that most writers would not have shared. But in her ministry of rescuing people at any cost, she did not spare the readers by trying to make her horrible experience light or easy on the readers' ears. She wanted to help others and to let them know that after the worst of things, God still has a deep calling and purpose on your life. Although He does not order the mess to be in your life, He flips the script and makes the mess a rescuing *message* and a way of escape for many.

Because of her openness in sharing, I trust she will cause many to see again their own great worth and value to the furtherance of the Message of the Kingdom. This book will be the added strength for rising from the ashes of assault to encouragement of continuing for so many. Many souls from around the world will be blessed by her boldness to expose the truth. Many would perhaps have chosen to try to save face—to keep up a good front—and would not have come out so boldly, or they would have been very malicious with exposure for payback. But from Theresa, we feel Christian love through this terrible dilemma. We see how she tried to hold something together that was not repairable because the other party didn't want it to be repaired. She kept a heart and spirit of forgiveness toward the other party to the point of belittling herself and almost losing any identity of herself. Yes, she hung in there and took it until she knew that it really had no resurrection life left in it even though she wanted it to. Yes, when she did all that she could do to stand, she endured the gut-wrenching hurt and kept standing and kept forgiving. We know that only the power of God could give her the strength to even nurse and care for that person after what she endured from him. But our Christ is the difference-maker who gives us the power to truly forgive.

I am grateful for being allowed to write the foreword to this well-written masterpiece of a life enduring for Christ through the worst of adverse circumstances and coming out of it with the joy of the Lord. May you, dear reader, take that joy to the world and help others to be delivered from any situation so they too will come out with great joy giving all the glory to Jesus. It was my honor to write the introduction to this amazing book.

Apostle Dr. Robert L. Jones
Pastor, Rivers of Living Water Ministries International

Foreword

THERESA MARIE IS A TRUE inspiration and prime example of standing on the promises written in the word of God, remaining steadfast at all times with unwavering faith, believing for the reconciliation of her marriage and family through the healing power of love and forgiveness. "Now faith is the substance of things hoped for, the evidence of things not seen" (Hebrews 11:1 KJV). This book is an honest and accurate account of Theresa's faith journey as she continued to preach through the pain while trusting in her God to do the miraculous in bringing restoration of her marriage. I truly believe this book will bring hope and healing to every heart, mind, soul, and spirit who has endured the gut-wrenching and heartbreaking betrayal of a spouse who is bound by the addiction of pornography. It is for those who have not only experienced the tragic destruction of the marriage covenant between husband and wife but the breakdown and dismantling of the family unit and the residual effects upon each child individually. I am grateful she had the courage to write this book, by sharing her story she is shining a light on the moral crisis facing our world today. May God's richest blessings be upon you as you read it.

Pastor Deborah Williams

Acknowledgments

I SURRENDERED MY LIFE TO MY Lord and Savior over thirty-nine years ago and I shall never cease thanking and praising Him for rescuing me. My journey in the Lord has been filled with the wondrous works of God in the best of times and the worst of times. Jesus never left me, nor forsook me. I am a living testimony of His strength being made strong in me while at my most vulnerable and weakest place. I wrote this book to share my testimony and encourage others that God will see you through the darkest seasons and He will enable you to forgive in order to heal. My testimony is not to condemn but to promote the power of forgiveness and Jesus' ability to heal the brokenhearted. May my story bring awareness to the body of Christ of the epidemic that has infiltrated the church and the world, along with the devastation it leaves behind.

I do not believe this is a book I can dedicate to anyone. I simply acknowledge my first love, Jesus, who has enabled me to complete this first book. I do not know where I would be without Jesus. He is my everything. To my children: my daughter, five sons, daughter-in-loves, son-in-love, seven grandchildren (and counting), and many other sons and daughters that call me mom ... I love you more than words could ever begin to express. You are the abundantly, above all, blessings that God has given me, and I am in awe of all of you. My heart still grieves that you had to experience the failed marriage of your parents, but I trust God to continue to heal your hearts and stand in faith that your legacies for your beautiful families will surpass your experience and God will be glorified in every area of your lives. To Deborah, Lawrence, Bishop, Pastor, Gina, Debra, Heidi, and Tina, who walked with me through this excruciating season and prayed for my family and me, and never spoke disparagingly but stood in faith for restoration and reconciliation, I am grateful beyond words. I will never forget your kindness, generosity, and love. To Gina, thank you for the design of the book cover and for encouraging the beginning of my writing journey. To my counselor, Dr. M, who helped me navigate through the darkness for over two years and "stay above the line," I thank you. I thank my editor and publisher for his patience and for making this process easy for me as a novice writer. I am grateful to my attorney who supported me through an excruciating time in my life. I thank him for his kindness, generosity, and fatherly advice through it all. I honor my mother who never said a disparaging word during this long season and whose heart also broke for my family and me, I thank you for loving me and giving me life. Finally, to Chris, thank you for your support and for encouraging me to complete the book I had begun writing before you ever entered my life, I thank you for loving me so well, I love you. To those I didn't know who prayed, interceded, and stood in faith for my family and me, I am grateful.

Theresa

Prologue

Be sober, be vigilant; because your adversary the devil, as a roaring lion, walketh about, seeking who he may devour; Whom resist steadfast in the faith, knowing that the same afflictions are experienced by your brethren that are in the world.

1 Peter 5:8–9 KJV

THE COURTROOM EMPTIED AS ALL the previous cases were heard. They called his name and the door behind the judge's bench opened. He entered the courtroom in shackles while wearing orange and white striped hospital-style pants and shirt. He had to shuffle to his place in the courtroom as the shackles appeared difficult to maneuver. He stood next to his attorney and listened to the charges.

"Domestic Violence in the 4th degree," said the judge. I stood there with my young-adult son regretting that I had allowed him to come with me to court and see his father like this. I thought, *How did this happen? How did the man I loved most of my life end up in shackles? How did the man that did prison ministry for years end up spending the weekend in jail and is now facing the judge? How does a man who preached the gospel seemingly be so far from what he was called to do? And how will our marriage survive?*

It was surreal and truly like watching a movie and not really happening. Was this just a bad dream? Will I wake up? Then I thought, *Maybe this is what it will take for him to turn back to God. To turn back to me, his wife and to turn back to our children. To walk in his true calling. Maybe this was hitting rock bottom finally.* But I was wrong and had no idea what was ahead.

It was one year after we had separated. I had left on a Friday night when I knew my younger two sons, who were older teens, would be attending a mission camp in Tennessee the next morning. They were already asleep at 11:30 PM and all packed for the morning. They would never know I was not home that night. I planned to text them in the morning, telling them to meet me for breakfast before going to the church to catch the vans to Tennessee. This would give me a week to figure out the answer to that nagging question: *Now what?*

That fateful Friday my husband had once again taken a day off work, and I knew nothing about it. He had left early in the morning, and I would have never known had I not let the dog out and saw the vehicle in the driveway picking him up at 7 AM. It was his buddy, his new best friend for the past two years, and I had no idea where they were going this time. I eventually found out that evening when the friend posted a picture on social media of himself on a golf cart surrounded by nearly a dozen young women in their thirties. My husband had taken the picture (there were more pictures taken that day that would later be discovered). They had gone to one of the islands on Lake Erie, a place known for a party atmosphere with plenty of alcohol and no boundaries in meeting new people of the opposite sex. I was hurt, furious, and I knew that was it. I had to leave or my anger would have destroyed his friend's car (at least, that is what I was feeling at time). This was just another betrayal on top of the mountain of betrayals.

I had overheard conversations between this friend and my husband where they spoke of other women and my husband even told him how he gave his number to the waitress at a restaurant who was "really into him and she was thirty-two with no baggage." Numerous other conversations were heard, as I had placed micro-recorders in his office and vehicle just a few weeks prior. I think if you get to a point where you are placing recorders in rooms or cars there is definitely a problem in your marriage. I am not saying that should be a normal procedure, but I chose to do that after wanting to discuss how I was feeling, what I was sensing, and even what I believed the Holy Spirit was telling me. I was vehemently denied any conversation to address the things that troubled me. I was told, "You are crazy," "take a pill for your menopause woman," "you can't tell me anything," "I don't have to answer your questions," and even the childish statement, "you are not the boss of me."

I had already discovered some of the porn he viewed on his phone and dealt with the hours missing from home, the days off work I knew nothing about, and the rumors circulating around the town we lived in about his indiscretions with tenants. I experienced being physically pushed out of our bed with two hands and being yelled at to get the *expletive* out of the bed because it was his room and bed. This happened one morning because of my refusing to have sex with him after he came home from his third-shift job and being berated the night before through text and voicemails while he was at work.

Just the month before, he threw lamps, tables, and pictures from our bedroom off the second-floor deck into the yard, destroying the newly purchased items I had acquired to spruce up our room. I had to wake my youngest son up in the midst of items being flung off the deck and tell him to get in the car, which still had a little trailer attached because I had been mowing lawns that day at rental properties. We spent that night at a hotel. My older son was at his senior prom that night and I knew he would be at a friend's home until morning for their after prom. The next day was Mother's Day—we had church and I had to preach the message. We were co-pastors at a church we had planted just three years prior.

I remember trying to be the "good Christian wife" and give myself to him whenever and however he wanted. I remember feeling and thinking that I would never measure up to the pictures I knew he was viewing and the way they performed the acts. I remembered feeling used, dirty, and unworthy. Yet, I knew the covenant of marriage was to be forever, for better or worse, in sickness and in health, 'til death do us part ... I just did not know that the death would be divorce. In the midst of the difficulty, I always felt I somehow failed my husband, that I was somehow not good enough, not satisfying enough. And truth be told, I felt I had failed God by not being a good enough wife.

I never responded with a demure tone at every new revelation I discovered. I would yell, I would cry, I would demand answers. I prayed and believed God for healing in our marriage, but for a length of time my responses to my husband's indiscretions were purely emotional and fleshly. It took the years during our separation to learn how to respond—or, more precisely, how *not* to respond—and trust God in the midst of deep emotional pain.

Chapter 1

The safest road to hell is the gradual one, the gentle slope, soft underfoot, without sudden turnings, without milestones, without signposts.

C.S. Lewis, *The Screwtape Letters*

THE PORN WAS DISCOVERED ON his phone two years prior to his arrest. My husband worked the night shift, driving for a prominent delivery company. He had always been an excellent provider, a man with a great work ethic who had worked for the company for over thirty-five years. He did not always work the night shift though, and I now look back and see how, when he chose to go to nights, that impacted our life insidiously.

I discovered the porn one summer evening when his phone rang, and it was charging in the kitchen. He was in bed upstairs, due to wake up in about an hour to leave for work. I got up to turn off his ringer, picked up the phone, and decided to look at who called. The Internet browser was also open and I could see the pages he had visited. I was totally blindsided when I saw "all naked women," "naked ladies," and numerous other search pages with images. I dropped the phone.

My first instinct was to go upstairs and scream at him to wake up. I knew how to yell (not saying this is right) and make my point. Instead, I just stayed downstairs in the family room. I cried for quite a while and pretended to be asleep on the couch when I heard him coming down to leave for work. I could hear him grab his phone and keys and walk out the door. Of course, he left without a kiss or even a verbal goodbye. I remember thinking, *When did that become the norm?* No goodbye, no kiss. You see, in a marriage, it is a slow fade to disconnect. Lack of kindness to one another, lack of affection, lack of communication, lack of self-control, lack of commitment—it doesn't happen overnight. The tearing apart begins with a small fringe, and before you know it each fringe is pulled and the fabric begins to unravel.

> It's a slow fade when you give yourself away
> It's a slow fade when black and white have turned to gray
> Thoughts invade, choices are made, a price will be paid
> When you give yourself away
> People never crumble in a day
> Daddies never crumble in a day
> Families never crumble in a day
> – "Slow Fade" lyrics by Casting Crowns

~

I confronted him the next day about what I had found on his phone. I asked him to come outside on the side porch to talk so the boys would not hear.

His first response was, "Why were you looking at my phone?"

I explained what had happened and that I was really not looking.

He then tried to explain how he was just looking for things for us as a couple and "that stuff just popped up."

I grilled him about "looking for things for us as a couple." What things?! I knew in my heart that was a deflection and a lie. We had a good sex life, to be honest (at least I thought we did), so "looking for things for us as a couple" would have been discussed between the two of us. He refused to discuss it. Furious, I grabbed his phone and smashed the screen on the brick pillar on our porch (again, an improper emotional response but it is exactly what I did in a fit of anger). I cried as I did it. I yelled at him, asking him, "How could you do this? Why did you do this? How long have you been looking at porn?"

His response was, "Just this once, it was an accident." And then he said "I am not dealing with you, and I don't have to answer your questions. I am leaving." He got in his car and left. I was furious. How could he leave me in that state? Could he not see my pain? Does he not see he betrayed me? How could he view porn while being a minister? I needed to talk this out. I was not O.K. with him leaving so I got in my car and tried to find him. I found him after about two hours. He was parked outside of an older man's home he had befriended.

I went up to the door and banged on it. Yes, banged on it. I could hear the older gentleman, who happened to be an alcoholic, yell, "Who the *expletive* is that?"

I responded, "It's -----'s wife!" My husband came to the door and opened it.

"What do you want?"

"What do I want?! I want to talk to you. I want you to answer me! I want to know how you think this is O.K.?"

He responded, "I don't have to talk to you, and you need to leave now!" And he slammed the door.

I began to cry and walked back to my car. As I walked by his vehicle, I could see another phone in it, plugged in to the charger. Just then I heard the door open. I reached in the open window of the car, grabbed the phone, and got in my car. He ran out and got in his car. He followed me the one and half miles home, honking the horn and yelling out the window, "Give me my phone!"

As I held the phone in my hand, I realized he had gone out and purchased another phone in that short period. I could not believe it. I got home, with him directly behind me. He began yelling at me, "Give me my phone. I bought it. It's not yours. I am calling the sheriff."

I said, "No, not until you talk to me. What are you hiding?" I stayed in my car and he took off in his. At that point I had to pick up my foster daughter. Yes, we were foster parents, we had been for twenty-five years. We provided a stable, loving home and had over 150 children come through our home over the years. Some of those children became our forever children, many others remain in our hearts, and many keep in regular contact. *This should not be happening*, is what I thought as I drove to pick up the child. We are Spirit-filled Christians, we are ministers, we are parents ... we love Jesus.

I picked up my foster child and drove back home where a sheriff's vehicle was waiting in my driveway. I could not believe it. He actually called the sheriff on me ... for real. I stopped the car and the sheriff walked up to my window. I told my foster child to go inside the house. My husband was sitting in his vehicle watching.

The sheriff asked if I had his phone. I said, "Yes." She informed me that it is his phone that he purchased himself. I responded that "we have a family phone plan, and all the phones are jointly owned."

She went back to talk to him, then returned and told me, "He got his own phone and account and if you return it to him, he said he will not press charges."

"Press charges?! I am his wife!" I yelled.

The deputy said, "He informed me you broke his other phone, and he will not press charges for that if you return his new phone."

"Did he tell you why I smashed his screen? Did he tell you the porn that was on his phone? Married over thirty years. How would you feel discovering that? Unbelievable." I handed the deputy the phone and it was returned to him. He pulled out of the driveway.

The deputy walked back over to my car and told me, "He won't be pressing charges and I advised him to stay away for a while until things cool down."

"He won't be pressing charges against his wife?! Who found porn on his phone ... wow, so nice of him!"

"Ma'am, I understand you are upset but it is best to have some distance until you two can talk reasonably."

The deputy left and I went into the house to talk to my 13-year-old foster daughter to try and explain why the sheriff was there without revealing to her the exact reason, but most importantly assuring her that there was no reason to be concerned and that she was safe. The irony of it all, she had dealt with so much and experienced officers at her home continuously. I was so upset that I would be part of this child experiencing anything similar.

How could he call the sheriff on me? I thought he loved me, would protect me, would lay his life down for me. He just threw me under the bus. Smashing his screen was not O.K. I acted out of hurt, anger, and what I felt was betrayal. Destroying property and having a lack of self-control is inexcusable. But where did he go? When will he be back? Will he talk to me so I can try and understand? Will we get through this?

~

It was about 11:30 PM and he had not returned. The three teens in the home were all asleep. I went out for a drive and went to the church, which was a couple of miles away. Often, I went to pray in my office and just be quiet before the Lord. When I pulled into the rear parking lot, his car was there. I opened the back door and went upstairs to where the office was. There he was on the couch.

"What are you doing?! Are you going to talk to me?!" I yelled.

He got up, grabbed his phone, and headed downstairs with me behind him yelling, "You can't just walk away! You need to answer me! Why did you do this? How long have you been looking at porn?! How could you call the police?!" You see, all I was focused on was the symptom of the issue and not the root or source. I took it personally and responded in my emotional pain.

I was right behind him, yelling and crying. He got to the doorway leading out back and turned around. All the while I was yelling and crying and just wanted acknowledgment. I could see something dark in his eyes and never imagined what he would do next.

He looked at me with such disgust and pushed me with both hands. I sprawled backward at least ten feet and fell to the floor after hitting a conference chair with wooden arms. He looked at me lying there with an expression of disbelief and then turned and walked out the door. I lay there in shock, but my back was really hurting, and I was afraid to move. The floor was concrete under thin commercial carpet. I was really hurt, and I just stayed on the floor.

After what seemed like about five minutes, my phone rang. I was just sitting up. It was my husband. "Are you O.K.?"

"I am not O.K. I am hurt. You pushed me across the room!" He hung up. I managed to get all the way up. It hurt when I walked. I went home and tried to sleep. The children were asleep and never knew what had just transpired or even that I had been gone. My husband never came home.

~

The next morning at about 6 AM I was in a lot of pain. I was scared and not sure how serious it was, so I decided to go to the emergency room. I am not one to run to the doctor for just anything, so for me to go to ER means I was really hurting. I had forgotten that this morning a group of men, some from the church and some from my husband's "friends' group" were going on a guy outing. They were all at a little local restaurant that I drove past on my way to the ER at 6:20 in the morning. I noticed my husband's car there as well as some others that I recognized. At the ER I checked in and was taken back to an exam room. As I waited, I thought to myself, *His friends have no idea what just happened last night. Or, maybe they do.* I wondered if he told them he never came home last night.

Just then the nurse came into the room and began to ask questions about how I hurt my back. I simply stated that I fell back into a wood armchair and hit the concrete floor. She actually asked if anyone was involved—a significant other, or a partner. I repeated that I fell back into a chair and hit the concrete floor. In my mind I was thinking, *I am covering for him, this is wrong.* I thought to myself, *If I were counseling anyone, I would tell them to tell the truth, tell the nurse, tell the police ...* DON'T COVER UP WRONG!

At the ER they took X-rays and nothing serious was discovered. The doctor told me it was a terrible bruise and that I would be sore for a while. He told me to watch for certain warning signs and if any occurred to come back to the ER immediately.

~

My husband came home that night. We didn't speak until the next morning. I was still very angry and told him we needed help. This was not O.K. He reluctantly agreed to meet with our assistant pastor and his wife. A meeting was set up for the following evening. We began to talk about what had transpired, with my husband saying that it was the first time he ever looked at porn and that it would not happen again. Then the assistant pastor confronted him about pushing me.

My husband became very angry and said, "I should have called the sheriff on her. She would have been arrested for yelling at me like that. She should not have come here."

The assistant pastor said, "She should not have been yelling like that, but that in no way gives you a right to push her. You are twice or three times as big as she is. You would have been arrested for pushing her. Did you know she went to the ER? Did you see her back?"

My husband stood up and said "I don't have to listen to this. I did nothing wrong. Big deal, I saw some naked pictures. I pushed her away from me, that is all," and he stomped out the door, slamming it.

We never discussed it again. He had said it was one time and would not happen again. Within three weeks he had a lock on his phone, and I was never permitted to look at it.

Chapter 2

For there is nothing hidden which will not be revealed, nor has anything been kept secret but that it should come to light.

Mark 4:22 NKJV

I BELIEVED I WAS DOING THE right thing by accepting what had transpired and forgiving. I committed to being long-suffering and remaining spiritual by just praying and trusting God would keep my family intact. What I did not realize at the time was that ignoring and not resolving the issues or setting boundaries only contributed to the worsening behaviors and continued the destruction of my family that I so badly wanted to protect. I thought I was protecting my children by doing damage control but later realized that isolating things would never fix the problem, it only enabled it to continue.

We owned some rental properties, and a few weeks after that first discovery of porn and the aftermath, I received texts from my husband late at night asking me to put a rental application on the porch for someone to pick up late that night. This was something I did not like doing, as this was our private home, and I did not like strangers and possible tenants to come there for business. But I went ahead and put the application on the porch as asked.

In the morning after the boys went off to school, I was working in the home office. I looked out on the porch and saw the application and some other papers, so I picked them up and looked at them. I recognized the name on the application. It was a woman who had recently friend-requested my husband on social media. At that time, I had access to his social media account only because I was the one who set it up for him and had used my new email address since he did not have one. I hadn't realized that I would then receive email notifications from the social media account.

I had asked him weeks prior when the friend request came in how he knew her or why she would request him. He said he didn't know. This woman was not someone I knew, but somehow, she knew my husband and was an "adult entertainment worker" which she put on her application, also known as a stripper. This was not the first odd friend request he received or a person he befriended on social media that was very much questionable for a married man, let alone a minister. Every time I would question such things it was rebutted with either, "None of your business," or, "I don't know how they got on my page."

I called him as I read the application and said, "This is the same woman who requested you on social media that you said you didn't know. She is a stripper. She has written a two-page explanation of how she is paid in cash for her adult entertainment job and requesting that you rent the apartment to her as you guys discussed." By that point I was yelling. He hung up.

There was a knock at the door immediately and to my surprise, it was the same woman standing there in my entryway. Here I was staring at the stripper "he didn't know" but she knows where we live and has spoken to my husband about renting an apartment.

I spoke with her and told her, "This is not a rental office. You will need to call for information."

She informed me she has been talking to my husband and thought she could just stop by. Imagine that. I called my husband after she left, and he did not answer. I was angry and at the same time felt compassion for the woman as I thought of her need for deliverance and salvation, and then felt guilty. I knew there was nothing too big for God and He forgives us all if we ask, and yet I was so caught up in my own feelings that I did not even pray for her. I do not know if he rented an apartment to her or what their relationship was, as he would never answer me about it.

~

We went along not discussing the elephant in the room. His phone was newly locked, the continued missing time after work, and not communicating what his plans were after work or even on the weekends. He began making more plans with male friends who were not married. Hanging out with them, going places. If I objected, I was called ungrateful (as he worked hard to provide for our family). I was told he doesn't have to answer my questions or tell me anything. He was the head of the household. We continued in ministry as co-pastors, but he began to preach fewer and fewer Sundays. He would converse with some of his friends during service who would show up to our ministry after they left their church (our church service began in the afternoon). He began going to their church before our services. Many times they would openly discuss the women at their church.

One particular day after our service was over, after I preached the message once again, they were laughing and talking in the corner of the sanctuary. I could hear him laughing and excitingly saying, "Did you see the lady down front in the white pants and black top? She is pretty. There's one for you buddy." They began discussing the women who attend that church, commenting on who was available, who was good-looking, who they would not mind going out with. He was the only married man in the conversation yet spoke as if he was also single like them.

He was the co-pastor of the church they were having this conversation in, and you would never know that, let alone that he was married.

I will admit that I was very insecure at that point. I do not think acknowledging the attractiveness of a female is a sin. I believe it is when the look becomes a second look or a lingering gaze then that may be an issue, especially when you are married. *Maybe my expectations are too high*, I often thought, and that conversing about women with single men is not a big deal. But something within me knew this is not O.K. The Holy Spirit within me was grieved. I oftentimes doubted what I discerned because of being told, "you're stupid," "you're menopausal, take a pill," "what an idiot." I was not some insecure teenager or young adult. I was over fifty and had walked with God, knew his voice and inklings from the Holy Spirit, but I would doubt it all, somehow thinking there really must be something wrong with me.

This was around the end of the summer and by March of the following year, there would be Sundays he never even showed up for church. We had a trip planned for the end of March for spring break. We went with another couple and our two youngest kids on a five-day cruise. I remember the Lord speaking to me that when I got off the boat I should be ready for a great battle and to continue preaching through the pain. I had no idea what that meant.

When we arrived home, we had some issues with one of our adult children who lived in a property that he rented from us. We received notice that the water bill was not paid. Instead of my husband calling our child to work it out, he called the water department and demanded the water be shut off so we would not be responsible for a delinquency bill. The major problem with that was that our child has a family and shutting off water meant our grandchildren had no water. The bill was only a few days late and a phone call to our child to ask when it would be paid would have been, in my opinion, the correct way to handle it. This caused much strife with our child and his family. There was already a strained relationship between him and his father, so it only added to the division. He paid the bill the next day and had the water turned back on but moved out of the home within weeks and did not speak to his father.

The difference in opinion on how the water bill should have been handled caused more strife in our relationship. As soon as we got home from vacation the patterns of behavior continued: not coming home after work with no communication as to what he was doing, phone locked, often on the phone in the other room, up at 4 AM on days off and leaving the house, evenings away, days off work that I knew nothing about. My husband continued to purchase more rental property and more vehicles without any discussion, and the cruel words continued. "You are so stupid," "you're menopausal so take a pill," "leave me alone," "none of your business you idiot."

I can remember writing in a journal shortly after we returned from that trip:

More Porn viewing discovered . . .
More secrets . . .
More lies . . .
What do you want from me Lord?!
The pain is deeper than I can feel . . .
Betrayal . . .
Aftermath of perversion?
Why do I feel unworthy, not good enough . . . ?
NOT LOVED!
Lord, help me ... just please help me get through this!!!
Help me be a better wife. Heal our marriage. Help my husband.

In my distress I called upon the Lord and cried unto my God: He heard my voice out of his temple, and my cry came before him even into his ears
– Psalm 18:6 KJV

Chapter 3

Leaving out details on purpose, half-truths, blatant lies ... is all lying.

The Lord detests lying lips, but he delights in people who are trustworthy.

Proverbs 12:22 NIV

I CAN LOOK BACK NOW AND see more clearly where things began to spiral downward. I remember four years prior to our initial separation my husband had a vacation week. On the first day of vacation, he was irritable. I responded right back with irritability saying to him, "If this is the way you are going to be while you are off this week then just go somewhere!" It definitely was not the right response, nor should I have said that.

He came downstairs within fifteen minutes with a bag in his hand and left. He was gone for three days, and I never knew where he went, he never called. At that time, we had locator apps on our phones, and I could locate him and see he was traveling out of state. It also happened to be over the 4th of July holiday. He returned home without a word. He expected us to be intimate the same night he returned and when I withdrew from his advances, he became angry. He held me down on the couch, turned me over, and started actually spanking me like a child, saying, "You deserve a good spanking. I am the head of this house." It was not done in foolish jesting; I was being held down against my will and he was actually hitting my butt.

I yelled for him to stop and reminded him there were children upstairs and said again, "Stop, please stop." He stopped and went upstairs. I slept on the couch. The next day he acted as if nothing happened. I tried to discuss what had happened, asked why he was gone for three days and never called (although I could have called him and did not), and why he thought that was an acceptable thing to do as a married man. I asked him if he was with someone ... he laughed and said no.

After that first incident of my husband being gone three days without his wife and family knowing where he was, it seemed to become easier for him not to come home after work, leave early (like 4 AM early) on Saturday and Sunday mornings and not return home until afternoon. That trip seemed to validate a lack of communication and that he was not obligated to tell me where he was going or about any plans he had made.

I became increasingly frustrated with this pattern. I know my response was not good—whether I screamed at him, "Where were you?!" or just gave him the silent treatment—it did not fix or change a thing. But the lack of consideration was evident. There were times he was kind and made plans for a night out, only to be followed by berating and anger the next day. We slept together and we had sex, but it seemed different than before. It felt as if it wasn't me he was making love to. I would try to verbalize how I felt, only to be dismissed and told over and over, "You're crazy," or asked, "You don't trust me?" and deflected which made me feel guilty: "I work hard for our family." I sensed with everything in me that something was off.

His anger was so visible when he was home. He let it show around me or even our two younger sons who were still in the house. When I observed him outside of the home, he was jovial, laughing, the life of the party. He had inside jokes with his new buddies. One of my sons later told me he spoke disparagingly about me to his friends at a men's breakfast and my son was quite shocked at what was shared. My husband continued to be gone at different hours. When it was late in the evening, I made sure I locked the kitchen door before going up to bed. He became angry with me about the door being locked, as he did not keep a key to the house on his key ring. There was, however, an accessible key in the garage, but he told me to not lock the door.

When I continued to lock the door he finally said, "If you lock the door again, I will bust it down." Busting it was exactly what he did. One evening at 11:30 PM I was heading up to bed. He had been gone all evening; my girlfriend was on the phone with me because I was upset once again about him being gone and I had no idea where he was. I locked the kitchen door and told my friend I was getting off the phone and going to try to go to sleep. At that moment I heard the doorknob rattle. My friend was still on the phone, and I told her he was home. I walked back into the kitchen to the sound of broken glass shattering and scattering across the floor.

He had taken a hammer to the window in the door and broke it so he could unlock the door. He walked in and said, "I told you not to lock the door again," and went upstairs to bed.

My friend, still on the phone, could hear everything. She was screaming at me, "Are you alright?! What is going on?!" I told her I was fine and explained what had just happened. She could hear the glass breaking and the sound of banging. She told me to call the police. I refused. I was so concerned about my sons and foster daughter hearing what just happened. Fortunately, where their bedrooms were located, they could not hear what was happening in the kitchen (at least I do not think they could). My friend came over after midnight to make sure I was O.K. She helped me clean up the glass and I taped a trash bag over the window.

When the kids got up in the morning, they asked what had happened. My response: "The glass broke last night." I covered for their dad again.

I called a contractor to have a new door put in the next day, but it would not get done for two days. At no time did my husband ask about the door, apologize for what he did, or say he would get it fixed. The person who repaired it and his wife were our friends and attended our church. They left the church shortly after that incident.

Chapter 4

When you pass through the waters, I will be with you; And through the rivers, they shall not overflow you. When you walk through the Fire, you shall not be burned, nor shall flame scorch you.

Isaiah 43:2 NKJV

THERE IS NO BETTER APOLOGY than changed behavior, no better repentance than humbly and honestly turning away from the sins you committed. But my husband continued to destroy my heart with words so painful all the while heading in the same direction. I had to learn love isn't all-accepting, all-tolerating, and all-allowing. Love has boundaries. I had to open my eyes to really see how continuing in the same direction may cause someone to begin loving things God hates. Sometimes the most loving thing you can do is to not accept someone's addiction, betrayal, lifestyle, or bad decisions. I knew it didn't happen overnight, as I clearly see looking back.

During those years of turmoil, I often felt as if I was looking at my life while being underwater with blurry eyes; everything was kind of blurry, but I could make out the shapes of the big things. I stumbled around, often feeling like I had failed God in some way. Yes, I continued to minister as I studied the word of God, prayed, and believed for change in my marriage. I prayed for others and encouraged them to hold on to their faith and saw God answer their prayers in many instances.

I felt shame often, wondering if I had taken the blessing of marriage for granted. I tried to not confront, to be meek, to continue to keep an immaculate home, and to keep the schedules of all the children. I cleaned a six-thousand-square-foot home by myself—although my children had chores, oftentimes their extracurricular activities did not leave much time for assisting in house-cleaning. Meals were always on the table; dishes were always done. I mowed the over-two-acre lot, trimmed, and landscaped. I mowed the rental properties and did the bookkeeping, leases, and other correspondence. I strived to be a godly wife but always felt I didn't measure up.

Maybe the words that I continually heard took root. I was often asked what I did all day. I felt I always had to be prepared with a list of things I had accomplished. Since I was primarily a stay-at-home mom, it appeared that I did not "work." Although I had many children in the home, attended meetings, took care of the house, and dinner was always made and ready, it seemed I had to prove my value. I assisted in the management of rentals on the administrative side but never handled the money. I would clean some rentals, mow many lawns, pick up materials, and file court papers, but somehow, I was still asked what I did all day. There were times when the children were in school, I would also work a part-time or even a seasonal full-time job and still maintain the responsibilities of the household and the rental business paperwork. My husband worked a job that was twelve hours a day. His schedule was third-shift so the responsibility of child-rearing, keeping the household, and attending school meetings were mine, as he rested during the day and worked through the night. He was a hard worker with a great work ethic but adding a business that grew exponentially had consequences.

All those things I did were never as important as our relationship. Again, unraveling doesn't happen overnight. The effort of all the responsibilities should have been sown into the marriage relationship. Nothing should have been allowed to infiltrate. We began the marriage founded on Jesus. When praying together began to become less frequent, it should have been noticed. When mutual respect and love began to wane, it should have been noticed. Nothing should have been allowed to separate or divide, but there is a devourer who lures the innocent and unsuspecting. He breaks hearts and shatters families. He will take his time to defile what is good and pure. He seeks to steal, kill, and destroy that which is good and holy (John 10:10).

Even a godly man.

Even a faithful wife.

Even a precious marriage.

~

My plan to stay faithful, maintain my marriage, and seek God to help me change my responses, reactions, and attitudes was the plan I was going to stay the course for. I believe God desired our marriage to be redeemed, restored, and reconciled. I was hopeful and expecting that we would remain in covenant as husband and wife. I realized during this long season that it takes two—and more importantly, it takes two with God as the center and leading us both. Unfortunately, unity in our marriage was not present.

Truly, I never expected betrayal and was not prepared for such grief and heartache. One thing I do know is that throughout this journey and long season, I sought God, and promised God that no matter the outcome I would serve Him. I know that God covered me, provided for me, and enabled me to forgive and be healed.

When your heart feels like it is broken into a million pieces and your world feels like it's completely unraveled, it can be difficult to see the light that is waiting at the end of the tunnel. Don't waste your time questioning why infidelity, addiction, and betrayal have ruined your relationship. Don't waste your time beating yourself up and questioning what is wrong with you, why was porn better, why you were not good enough. Instead, look up to where your help comes from and know you can face the world because God will provide anything and everything that you may need to overcome the pain. You will not just survive but thrive in Christ Jesus. God knows what it will take to heal and be whole. Trust God and be patient believing that he will complete what he began in you.

> Heal me, O Lord, and I shall be healed, save me.
> And I shall be saved; for you are my praise.
> – Jeremiah 17:14 NKJV

I continued to pray and seek God, but often felt shame and hid my fear. The failure shook my faith, my confidence, and forced me to reexamine both.

I experienced a spiritual battle as much as a mental one.

I saw how the enemy was trying to use shame to defeat me.

I had to determine to conquer the enemy who wanted to conquer me, to surrender my fears to God and the truth that He is in control. Then I had to go to war within myself—war against shame and anxiety and cast all fears out.

The enemy of our souls would like nothing else than for you and me to not fulfill that for which we're made.

We must defeat fear with faith ... and facts. Whatever the struggle, there is a solution available to you. It is grounded in the truth of God's Word. His Word is truth.

He has a purpose that you and I are meant to fulfill and there is always hope!

Faith combined with hope makes for a better day!

It doesn't matter if you are a faithful Christian or not, trouble and trials are inevitable. It is not a matter of if, but when. I am convinced that none of us are exempt from the storms of life.

Chapter 5

But my God shall supply all your need according to his riches in glory by Christ Jesus.

Philippians 4:19 KJV

MY HUSBAND WAS RELEASED THAT day at court when the charges were read. A hearing was scheduled in the next few weeks. He returned to the condo he had purchased just three months after we separated which was fifty minutes from where we lived. I returned home with my two younger sons. At this point, we had been separated for thirteen months. I filed for legal separation three weeks after I left that evening of his trip to Lake Erie Island and the social media post by his friend. I painfully decided to include the words "to reconcile" and "attend counseling" in the separation filing.

I had no means of support being a stay-at-home mother most of our marriage, and the voicemails I began receiving were so full of profanity and guile, I honestly was afraid of where it was all going. I became so accustomed to hearing the words and not acknowledging the effect they had on my heart, my mind, and my spirit: "You are a wrinkled up, old bag, no one would want you. You will never have a man as good as me. I am the best thing that ever happened to you. You would have been nothing without me."

I moved into an empty home we had that my daughter and son-in-law were going to rent until they purchased another home. My two younger sons and I lived there with them for four months and they provided for us. I got a job as a server at a new restaurant to help with utilities at least, but they fed and housed us as my husband did not give any financial aid. Two years prior, my husband began putting all of the money into his personal account which left me with no access to funds. I used credit cards for two years to purchase food, clothes, and Christmas and birthday gifts. The minimum required credit card payments were made by my husband, but he continued to keep all of the income and never asked how I was buying things for Christmas or even weekly groceries. I guess he assumed I used the credit cards and that his minimum payment was enough, which clearly would have been denial. I would tell him we needed to stop getting in debt. I had no clue he had acquired more debt than I knew of.

The month before I finally left and filed for separation was our high-school-aged son's graduation party. We had a food truck cater the event and my husband had me write the check for the caterer. I later found out from the sheriff's office that he accused me of stealing money from his account by writing that check. He was told we are legally "married," and a wife can't steal from her husband even though it was his individual account. I realized now that infidelity comes in many forms, including financial infidelity and sexual infidelity. As the good wife, I was not to question anything, not to ask where the money was going or how we could afford another property. Paying for our son's college tuition balance was a struggle. I put his first payment on a credit card. I later found out during the court hearing for separation that there were two more credit cards taken out in my name that I knew nothing about. They were maxed out.

At our first separation hearing, I was granted the marital home, and my youngest son and I were to move back within weeks. Unfortunately, before that happened, my husband began throwing trash in the front yard of our home, he began emptying the home of all the furniture, and he threw my clothes, shoes, boots, and purses away (I had only taken bare necessities when I left that summer), and now the weather was getting colder. One of his "friends" informed me that some of my shoes may be at goodwill. The humiliation of going to goodwill and asking to look through the large donation bins in the rear was overwhelming. I found quite a few pairs of my shoes but nothing else. All my boots were gone. I will say that God has replaced those boots, shoes, and purses that were lost exceedingly and abundantly above what I could ever imagine. It seemed people were giving me boots and purses left and right. I would come across things for next to nothing that were better than the shoes I had. God provided continuously and I was never forsaken.

Initially, my husband refused to allow us to move back home, and another hearing was set. The judge was informed that all the items had been taken from the home and it was almost empty. I am talking about a 6,000-square-foot home with another 3,000-square-foot attic. The home had been full of antiques and furniture acquired over the years. He was ordered to return all the items and my son and I moved back in. Financial support was also ordered after 5 months. It was like setting up a house all over again as everything was a mess, the walls were empty, rooms were piled with returned items, and mice had moved in. I was able to put it all back in order and continued to hope and pray for restoration.

I had filed for legal separation and in the filing, it stated the hope for counseling and reconciliation, and I would continue to hold on to hope for that to come to fruition. My attorney told me that no one files for separation anymore. I told my attorney, "I am a Christian who believes in fighting for her marriage, and I am hoping and praying our marriage will be restored."

I had left on a Friday night (after the social media post) and my husband did not even realize I was gone until Monday. There were so many things that transpired in the first few months of our separation before a hearing even happened. My husband took my college-aged son's car and threatened to call the police on him. My husband took another vehicle I had that the same son was driving to his summer job and his boots and uniform were in there. There was just no consideration for anyone else around him.

I requested a police escort (at my attorney's recommendation) for my sons and me to get some of their things from the home and also the things from the vehicle. When we arrived with the escort, my husband let us in, and sitting on the kitchen island was a semiautomatic handgun. The officer asked if it was loaded. My husband replied yes. The officer picked it up and looked at it and placed it back on the counter. My sons went upstairs to obtain things from their rooms, and I remained in the kitchen with the officer. When questioned about the gun my husband laughed and said, "I can have a loaded gun in my own home." I was shocked. My husband did not know I had called for an escort to the home, he only knew we were coming by for my sons to pick up a few things. I am sure thankful I heeded the attorney's advice to have the escort.

I remember while living with my daughter and her husband, about two months after separating and before our first court date, my husband invited me to go to Lake Erie and talk. I did not want to but one of my sons actually encouraged me to go, so I agreed even though my spirit was troubled. It did not take long before the talking became arguments, especially when his friend was calling and texting while we were there. At that time, I had not learned that no response is best, and I reacted and responded in anger, yelling, and demanding he put the phone away. My outburst helped nothing, but in no way justified that I ended up being left in a Lake Erie hotel room after the argument because I refused to agree to the order, "I will give you a ride back if you get in the car and shut the *expletive* up and don't say a word until we get home." He sent me texts full of profanity and vulgarity that night as I waited for a ride home. One of my good friends drove five hours round trip to pick me up and take me home.

Both of my sons were living with me at my daughter's home, and they were involved in youth group. There were outings that summer that cost money and God always provided always through so many people. It was a humbling experience to be a receiver and not the giver. I cried so many times at God's on-time provisions. I was working at the restaurant but that did not make a dent in the bills (credit cards) that were in my name. Somehow, they were always paid on time. God provided and I stopped trying to figure it out.

Chapter 6

You are my hiding place and my shield. I have put my hope in your word.

Psalm 119:114 BSB

After the Lake Erie fiasco, I discovered the $500 check he gave me the week prior (the only check he gave me at that point) did not clear. I needed funds for my sons' upcoming mission trip deposits. I went to the marital home out of frustration to discuss the check. He did not answer the door which was probably for the best. His car was not there but another of his vehicles was. I looked in the window and saw his phone. The door was unlocked, and I took the phone hoping it was unlocked, with the intent to look at it and then return it. I drove down the street to look at it away from the property in case he returned. When I say I saw his phone, I honestly thought it was "his phone." I took it hoping it was unlocked so I could see if there were more indiscretions on it. He had been saying he was no longer "doing that."

The phone was unlocked, and I could not believe it. He had kept his phone locked for about two years at this point. It was weird because it was unlocked and there was a strange text from his "friend" that said, "I saved your new number as ----." I thought to myself, *New number*? I pulled down the screen from the top and realized that this was another phone, not his primary phone—an identical phone but with a different number.

I discovered forty-eight pages of porn left open on the phone. I saw things I wished I had never seen. Websites of all types of porn were open. So many disturbing titles on each page. I thought I was going to be sick. My stomach turned, I was lightheaded, and could not believe what was on the phone. I never really imagined how bad porn really was. I realized the first time I saw it on his "real phone" was over 2 years prior. He actually had a second phone to view porn. I discovered my husband had been receiving pictures from women he did not know. He was on sites where you can "hook up with a local woman tonight." Did he? How far did this progress?

I called a good friend from the parking lot crying and she could hardly understand what I was saying. There were only three people whom I truly confided in with details of what was happening in my marriage and separation. They were people who would pray and believe God for deliverance and restoration. I took the phone home. He never knew I had it. As a matter of fact, he called the phone while I had it, obviously looking for it.

Pornography in all forms is an epidemic in our society. It's a secret addiction for many and a stronghold even in the Church. Statistics are staggering. The aftermath has reached far in the destruction of marriage, families, and communities. It changes the mindsets of all those involved and opens doors to more perversion and other demonic influences. The reality is that my situation is not an isolated case. Jesus is still the answer. Jesus still delivers the captives. The body of Christ needs to be praying. We cannot be surprised when the things of this world are accomplished in our brethren. I know in my heart that Jesus did not come to just fix the symptoms, but he wants to break the cycle.

I agreed to see my husband about a week later, on a Sunday evening, to talk. I was attending a church service and was to meet him afterward, but he decided to come to the service. That would be the first time he met the pastor at this church. This pastor had already had me speak on two different occasions for special services he had. We had (I thought) a good ministerial relationship with mutual respect. After all, he had invited me to speak at his church and thanked me both times for the word that I brought forth. I will share more about that later.

We drove together afterward as he had ridden with a friend to the church. I then addressed the new phone and what I had discovered very calmly and directly. He immediately became defensive and said he only did that because he was mad at me. Then he said, "Well, I knew you were looking at my phone, that is why I had that on there."

I reminded him this was his second phone that I didn't know he had. I also calmly stated, "I can see your data usage on your 'real phone' ... it is very high, so you are on the Internet a lot."

He did not deny it further but deflected onto me: "You would not have sex with me," (although we had an active sex life until we separated just eight weeks prior, and even during that time we had been intimate), "You made me mad."

I asked about the horrible sites I saw and how he could think that was acceptable. He would not answer. I dropped him off and went back to my daughter's. When I got home, he texted me to bring back the phone, or once again he would call the sheriff (the county sheriff's department was called more times than I care to remember). I took pictures of the Internet history and all the sites and drove back to the home and threw the phone on the porch and left. The question in my mind was, *How long did he have two phones?*

In spite of finding the second phone, I told myself I was standing in faith and believing God to restore my marriage. I thought I forgave; I chose to forgive. I began receiving texts in the middle of the night, often asking me to come to the house on the weekend. I had to turn off my phone at night. Texts usually started nice, then when I did not respond they would abruptly change to the most profane and emotionally destroying words. I would wake up and see the texts and many times would become physically sick.

I continued to pray and seek God, but out of shame I hid my fear. This betrayal shook my faith as well as my confidence and forced me to reexamine both. I was experiencing a spiritual battle as much as a mental one, and I saw that Satan was trying to use shame to defeat me. I had to determine to defeat the enemy and to stand on the word of God.

> Yet in all these things we [I] are more than conquerors through Him who loved us [me].
> – Romans 8:37 NKJV

I had to surrender my fears to God and trust that He is in control. I went to war with my anxiety and my shame and began to cast out all those fears. I would need to conquer fear daily and the only way was through faith. Faith comes by hearing and hearing by the word of God (Romans 10:17). I knew there was a solution through Jesus. I knew God has a purpose that I must fulfill and that there is always hope. I made up my mind daily and sometimes hourly to combine hope with faith and trust things to get better. So, I decided to cry if needed but that I would dry those tears when I was done, shake it off, get a grip on God again, and keep moving forward. I knew God was still in control.

Here is a journal entry from around the time of the Lake Erie fiasco:

Be still and know that I am God . . .

I will strive to be still Lord, to trust you.

Holding on to full restoration of my entire family.

My husband and I are one in you Lord.

Love that never fails, Agape transcended into our life together

Rebuke the devourer Lord. Reach far Lord and draw your children back to you.

Every distraction, evil influence, ungodly word, curse be broken over our marriage and family. SET FREE.

Chapter 7

When my spirit was overwhelmed within me, then thou knewest my path.

Psalm 142:3a KJV

DURING THE SECOND MONTH OF our separation, one of my sons had emergency surgery. It was a serious thing and I'm thankful how in the midst of all that was going on God answered our prayers. My son was fine and would recover more than well (a miracle, really). My husband came to the hospital. While my son was hospitalized, I stayed all night the first two nights. The morning I was to go home and get cleaned up, my husband wanted me to come home with him. I chose to go to my daughter's home where I was still staying at that time. I began receiving unkind texts again, as he wanted us to be intimate and I did not oblige. I had been at the hospital with our son for two nights and was exhausted. I ignored the texts. I had a cycle of blocking and unblocking his phone number during our nearly four-year separation. It was difficult to keep it blocked because we had children, and I became accustomed to, and almost felt deserving of the berating I would regularly receive. It was toxic and abusive, and my mind needed to be renewed. God does not require anyone to accept or receive words that bring death or that curse you. I equated forgiveness with accepting the behavior and continued in the cycle.

Forgiveness is immediate, or it should be, but *trust* must be earned, and I never could separate that. As a Christian woman and wife, I truly believed I was to bear this betrayal, or I was not forgiving. I did not realize that trust was broken, and to rebuild trust would take consistent behavior that gave evidence of a changed heart—a fruit of repentance.

> Therefore bear fruits worthy of repentance.
> - Matthew 3:8 NKJV

I believe in growing in grace and wisdom. Grace means extending others forgiveness, just as God extended it to you. Wisdom means being able to discern what kind of relationship you can have with a person in the future. Restoration of a broken relationship needs evidence of repentance, which includes a consistent pattern of changed behavior. It took me time to receive this knowledge and act accordingly without continuing to make excuses and accept the behaviors that were contrary to that of someone who truly repented and desired restoration.

Three months after our initial separation I discovered that money was missing from the ministry bank account. I was continuing to have Sunday services and the ministry took up offerings. It was a small ministry, so we are not talking about a lot of money. I had gone into the bank to make a deposit (all offerings were counted by two people who took up the offering and recorded the amount). I only made deposits and wrote checks for bills or outreach. I was the only approved signer for checks. I discovered that the balance in my checkbook and the balance the bank showed were different. The manager took me into her office and gave me a printout. I looked at the printout and saw a cash withdrawal of $1,800. The ministry never made cash withdrawals. All accounting was done with checks and balances: checks written, receipts, etc. She went back to see who made the cash withdrawal and discovered it was my husband. He was not previously a signer on the checking account, but he had gone in the week before to become one. Because the ministry was founded by both of us, he was allowed to do so. The problem was that our bylaws did not permit cash withdrawals without approval from board members. Not knowing that a large amount of money was withdrawn could have caused many checks to not clear, and we had never written a bad check or paid ministry bills late.

My husband had not been coming to church since the end of April, and this was in August. There was no reason to remove funds without permission or notification. I was furious and upset. I began crying in the bank manager's office. This was a local bank that we had used for numerous years for ministry and business. I called my husband after leaving the bank and he said, "It's marital property."

I told him it is not marital property as the ministry was a 501(c)(3) and that money did not belong to us personally. After getting nowhere in our conversation, and him refusing to return the money to the ministry, I was forced to file a police report on behalf of the ministry. The police investigated and called me after being told by a board member—who was also my husband's friend—that he had told him he was going to take money out of account. That board member had never informed the other board members or me as the co-pastor and only acting pastor at the church at that point. The board member was dismissed from the board as a result. My husband was then sent a letter from the ministry and remaining board members requesting him to re-engage as co-pastor and be restored. It was the board members' desire that he be fully restored by God, as we believe God can restore the fallen; God redeems, and most importantly God forgives because of Jesus.

My husband would not comply with the request. He continued to not attend except sporadically. Sometimes he would show up and go up to the pulpit if there was an opportunity and grab a mic, or he would sit in the congregation, make comments, and mock the sermon. We had to hold the mic so it would not be accessible. The ministry never banned him from coming in but desired that he would attend and hoped and prayed this would cause transformation and reason would return to him. My husband was ordered by the judge at our first hearing to return the money to the ministry. He complied and the ministry dropped the civil suit that had been filed to get funds back.

I truly believe God intervened so the ministry would know money was gone and we would not write any bad checks. God provided for the needs of the ministry. Our outreach and benevolence for that year was 90% of our income. God is a God of multiplication. The ministry was about outreach and helping others. The ministry paid for utility bills for numerous people who experienced hard times, bought groceries for many, paid for gas and doctor bills, and helped with rent and car repairs. You can never outgive God!

After the bank incident with the ministry funds, the bank would not close on two properties my husband was trying to purchase during our separation. The manager at the bank had heard what had happened, and our separation caused a greater risk. This bank held the mortgages on more than half of the forty properties in our names. They would not agree to close on these loans without us both in agreement. In the past, my husband had been able to close on loans without my consent. He was livid. I began receiving voicemails and texts. Besides calling me names, he stated he wanted a divorce ASAP. This was just three months into our separation.

His inability to purchase property when he wanted caused great anger. Rental property was a priority in his life, and it had not mattered for a long time how I felt about it. He was acquiring so many units he could not keep up with the maintenance, and his reputation in our town was not good as a landlord. It was embarrassing to hear the opinions, rumors, and social media posts about the conditions of some of the properties and the responses from my husband. Having rentals caused many disagreements. I was a firm believer that if you have rental property, it should be cared for and rented in a condition that you yourself would live in. We disagreed on that premise. I was appalled at the condition of many of the properties and that he would rent them in that condition. I had no say in any of it. His reputation as a landlord continued to decline. It affected our children too.

> A good name is to be chosen rather than great riches, loving favor rather than silver and gold.
> – Proverbs 22:1 NKJV

I truly believe continuing to acquire rental property was a significant part of the destruction of our marriage. It opened doors to other forms of destruction. Addiction comes in all forms.

Chapter 8

For thou art my hope, O Lord God: thou art my trust from my youth.

Psalm 71:5 KJV

Thou hast shewed me great and severe troubles, shalt revive me again, and shall bring me up again from the depths of the earth.

Psalm 71:20 KJV

In the fall, five months after our initial separation, I moved back into our home and my husband had already moved fifty minutes away to a condo he had purchased in the city. Maintenance support had been ordered, and the judge had also ordered that rental income be put in a joint account and all transactions recorded. My husband did not like this as it would mean I also saw the rents deposited, there would be no cash withdrawals, and all bills had to be paid via check or check card so there was accountability. My husband turned it all over to me. I was already used to doing the bookkeeping, but it was only based on what figures he told me, some receipts, and the amounts of rent paid. I never saw cash, nor did I write the checks. Now I was writing checks, arranging for maintenance, as well as handling the applications, leases, and lawn care. It was interesting to see just how much the rentals cost and how much money came in every month. I could also see how overextended we really were. It was a constant shuffle, as with that many units there were vacancies, non-payment of rent, and unexpected maintenance issues. All household bills were ordered to be paid out of that joint account as well. This included the mortgage, utilities, and taxes. I ended up handling this myself for six months and into the spring.

I spent Thanksgiving and Christmas back in the marital home. It was the kids' first Thanksgiving without their father there and it was difficult. I knew my children were grieving and I felt responsible and helpless at the same time. Near Christmastime, I told my children their dad was welcome to come over on Christmas Eve, as we had a tradition to have an open house for our family and friends after the Christmas Eve Service. The children and I assumed he would be there. The Christmas Eve Service was to begin at 6:30. I would be giving a short message and we would have worship songs celebrating the birth of Jesus.

At 6:15, my youngest son came over to me to show me his phone and a text he had received from his father. It said, "Guess where I am." My son responded, "I don't know." And his father replied with a picture of the ocean and stated, "In Florida." Their father went to Florida without telling them and spent over a week there, missing Christmas. My children were visibly grieved and once again I felt responsible and could not change a thing. I dealt with the fact that I was the one who filed for separation and if I had not, their father would at least still be present for the holidays and join in the family traditions. *How could I do this to my kids? Maybe I should not have filed. Should I have just continued the way things were and continued just praying and believing? What have I done? Will my children hate me?* At that point, I doubted everything, including myself. I was willing to endure the infidelity, lies, berating, anger, and financial betrayal for my children to be O.K. I sought the Lord, I cried, I repented and asked God if I was wrong, I talked to my counselor, I cried some more.

One of the worst things you can do as a Christian is to go around with this mask on, saying, "I love God and He is Good," when your heart is breaking inside, and I had been doing that for a very long time. I came to realize that you can say, "God is good," with tears running down your cheeks because He will see you through and He never wastes your sorrows. I learned I did not have to pretend anymore and trusted God that by His magnificent power, He would transform my sorrows and use all things for my good. I held on to His unfailing strength in the sorrow.

For my power is made perfect in weakness.
- 2 Corinthians 12:9 NIV

After the first of the year, after his return from Florida, my husband agreed to begin attending counseling with me. I had tried to ask him about his trip, whether he was alone, and he had done. He refused to answer any questions. To this day he is "friends" with a woman he met while there and he never told me what may or may not have happened. I should have realized then that someone who desires his marriage to be restored would not take off on a vacation alone during the holidays. I chose to forgive and dealt with my suspicions by giving them to God (this is what I believed I was to do) and not think about them.

I was already in counseling with a wonderful Christian doctor. It was supposed to be marital counseling from the beginning, but since my husband had refused to come for three months, it was individual counseling for me and I am grateful I had that guidance and assistance to heal since I did not know what was ahead at that point. We were six months into our initial separation when he finally agreed to come to counseling. He was living in his condominium away from everyone and the rentals, I was in the marital home with our youngest son, and our college-aged son would come home on breaks. I was still handling all the responsibilities of the rental properties.

My husband and I continued the cycle of seeing one another and then within days it would regress, and I would be discarded. The business had grown to be more than could be handled by a husband with a full-time job of more than sixty hours a week and a wife who was home with children and foster children, co-pastoring a ministry, and continuing to study in order to be prepared to preach and teach. Now, understand I do not think owning rental property is bad or sinful but what I did learn, observe, and experience is that God can bless and lead us to obtain possessions, but there are times when we get ahead of God or make decisions without His approval and those decisions have consequences. Every action has a reaction. Every decision has a consequence, good or bad.

The acquisition of property became like an addiction for my husband. It seemed like it was the art of the deal: making an offer, getting a good deal, adding to the portfolio, and calling it a blessing. A *blessing at what cost?* I often wondered. Time away from family, more responsibility, more debt, more stress. You can never get time back. What was the true calling for my husband? Rentals or ministry? Can you do both? I believe you can, but I also believe the enemy will lay traps and snares that look good and seemingly have a good outcome, but in the end lead to destruction. Addiction comes in many forms and can lead to other addictions.

While still separated and standing in faith for restoration, I believed God would deliver and heal our marriage and restore all that the enemy had tried to steal, kill, and destroy. With my stance on faith, I somehow believed I should continue the cycle. He would call me or text me and be kind, ask me to go to dinner, and inevitably it would lead to intimacy. EVERY. SINGLE. TIME. And each time less than three days later the anger, rage, and berating would begin. It left me devastated, feeling used and abused. I was called names for sleeping with my husband and then he would apologize only to begin the cycle again. There were times I blocked his number and then unblocked it and this toxic, dysfunctional behavior I partook in never allowed healing or restoration, and I now realize this.

~

There was one time when he had left his vehicle at the marital home and took his truck back to his condo. I needed an umbrella and remembered there was one in the hatch of that vehicle. As I opened the vehicle I also looked around before getting in the hatch. There was nothing unusual and I was relieved. I got the umbrella out of the rear hatchback and then noticed the covering was moved that covered the storage underneath. I lifted that cover and discovered a plastic bag in the storage area. I opened the bag that was a little heavy and filled with something that I honestly at first did not comprehend what it was. Inside the bag were many rubber-like devices, some battery-powered, in different shapes, some of which resembled a male body part. I realized they were used for sexual acts. There was scented lubrication and a spray cleaner made specifically for these items. To say I was shocked was an understatement. I took the bag inside and took a picture of the items. I sent the picture to my husband and asked why he had these items, what he did with these items, and who he used them on. Then I called him and I was so upset and beside myself. I was sick to my stomach and so many thoughts and scenarios ran through my head. Once again, he deflected onto me. He said I should have not been rummaging through his vehicle (which was once our family vehicle—that's how I knew there was an umbrella in it) and that it was none of my business. He hung up on me and I called back, and he finally said they were items left at a rental and he thought it was funny.

I called him out and asked, "So you picked up used sexual apparatuses, and you were going to do what with them?"

He began laughing and said he just thought it was funny. I told him how disgusting to even touch used items like that, let alone keep them and hide them in the hidden storage area in the rear of the vehicle. He once again deflected, said I was a snoop and out of my mind, and hung up on me but not before telling me to put it back in his vehicle. We did not speak for a few days, but once again he convinced me it was all a mistake and I overreacted, and he threw all that stuff away. And just like that, I got back into the cycle of dysfunction and somehow reasoned the whole incident away. I wanted my marriage to be restored and was willing to overlook so many things but that was not going to bring about true restoration or reconciliation. Denial never enables deliverance; it only causes bondage to continue.

Chapter 9

But I say unto you which hear, love your enemies, do good to them which hate you, bless them that curse you, and pray for them which despitefully use you.

Luke 6:27-28 NKJV

THERE CAME A POINT EARLY in the year that he started attending counseling and told me he was no longer viewing porn, talking to other women, etc., and that he would do anything to restore our marriage for us to reconcile. He came to counseling three weeks in a row. Things seemed to change, and we talked about how he would move back home and what the next steps would be. He asked me to drop the separation, and he would sell the condominium and come home. He begged me to drop it because he loved me and wanted no one else. I called my attorney and told him to file the papers to drop it. My attorney tried to advise me to give it time. I insisted my husband was going to counseling (even though it had only been three weeks), that financial accountability was in place with the joint account, and reminded my attorney (who was also a Christian) that I was a Christian woman who did not believe in divorce but believed my marriage would be restored. So, by March (nine months after the initial separation) the legal separation filing was dismissed by me. Dropping the separation also meant no longer receiving court-ordered support. By the beginning of April, my husband stopped coming to counseling. I discovered he still had his second phone at his condominium which he was able to continue to view porn on, and he began collecting rents and not depositing them into the joint account for accountability. He took over all the rental property again and would just have me type up leases and notices and do bookkeeping without seeing any funds.

He once again had all control over all the money. The decision to drop the legal separation left me with no real income. I was able to speak with the tenants that lived in the rear of the marital home property to have them pay me directly. This enabled me to pay all the bills in my name, but it did not cover groceries, gas, and other needs for my fifteen-year-old son. I started working as a front desk reservation clerk and we continued to live separately. He laughed at me when I asked how he could lie to me. "You said you would go to counseling, that you wanted to restore our marriage," I said. As I look back, I can see it was all about control, and more about financial control than anything else. The needs of our youngest son, or for that matter our son in his first year of college, were not even considered. He was not forced to support us in any way, and he didn't.

After discovering he still had the second phone and seeing the Internet history that progressed into hookup sites, escort services, and other perverse sites, we went weeks without talking to or seeing one another. I was beginning to learn to not respond in my flesh or feelings. I began to truly learn to cast it all at Jesus' feet. To cast all the burden and the pain on God, for I knew he cared for me (1 Peter 5:7). I began to not respond impulsively with my mouth, but to pray—pray for my son, pray for my adult children, pray for myself, and pray for my husband. I still believed God was able. There were times I could feel my heart in a million pieces, and it would take my breath away. I would literally fall to my knees and cry out to God. I always felt God's presence, but it did not take away the grief. His presence just enabled me to go through it and receive his peace.

There were times my husband's friends would seemingly be used by the enemy. They would either post things on social media showing my husband with them at places with women, or just post memes that were contrary to marriage. There were times some of them would comment on social media about me. The ministry included a radio program on which I hosted guests, and one of his friends even contacted one of my radio guests and advised them not to be my guest. He gave them his take on what was going on in our marriage. These things brought me to my knees also. I did not always respond well.

One instance was when my son who was in college was attending a church near campus and his father showed up to visit with one of these friends. This was the same friend that posted the initial picture of them with other women on social media. He posted a picture of them at the church where my son was attending on social media, and I commented all in my flesh. My comment mentioned the porn viewing and asked if they watched it together before church. It was wrong, it was inappropriate, and I had to repent after I deleted it. There were other times I responded just as badly, but I eventually learned to not respond and have self-control. It was not easy, but I leaned on the Lord and asked him to help me, to strengthen me, and to teach me to refrain from speaking. I learned what self-control truly is, but it was only through God. I remember coming to the place of praying for those men fervently, acknowledging that they did not know what they were doing, and choosing to forgive them. It was then that I realized—because I was not responding to them anymore and genuinely praying for them—that I had forgiven them.

> In my distress I called to the Lord; I cried to my God for help. From His temple He heard my voice; my cry came before Him ... He reached down from

on high and took hold of me; He drew me out of deep waters. He rescued me from my powerful enemy, from my foes, who were too strong for me. They confronted me in the day of my disaster, but the Lord was my support.
– Psalm 18:6, 16-18 NIV

Chapter 10

At every moment I called out to you, you answered me! You strengthened me deep within my soul and breathed fresh courage into me.

Psalm 138:3 TPT

In mid-June, one year after the initial separation and two months after I dropped the filing for legal separation, my husband came to the marital home. I had a garage sale that day for a mother who had downsized and moved to a smaller place. We were finishing cleaning up and I went upstairs to change and get ready to go to a friend's graduation party for her daughter when my 15-year-old son came banging on my bedroom door. I opened the door and saw him standing there shaking and holding a baseball bat at his side.

He said, "Dad's in the house, I think. He broke windows."

I came downstairs to discover two windows broken by plants in pots, which were thrown into the house from the outside. I could hear my husband yelling "OPEN THE DOOR OR ELSE!" I think I was in shock looking at the glass and large planters in the kitchen and dining room.

My son was standing behind me and said, "Call 911."

I said, "I don't have my phone." But my son had his and he dialed 911 and handed me the phone. The dispatcher on the other line could hear yelling. She said she would stay on the line until the deputies got there. I told her I could hear my husband coming up the steps to the kitchen door and I was unlocking it because I could not afford to repair anything else. I was not prepared for what I would see. I unlocked the door and saw my husband standing there with a pickaxe in his hand. He came into the kitchen with it. My son was standing behind me and telling him to get out, still holding the bat by his side. My husband lifted the pickaxe to his waist, and I could see the rage in his eyes. I was petrified and only thought, *If someone is getting hurt or worse, let it be me.*

I sternly told my son, "GO UPSTAIRS NOW!"

My son said, "No," at first, and I repeated myself—not yelling but sternly—and he went around to the steps. I looked at my husband and said as bravely and confidently as I could, "Stop. You need to leave now." I did not want to appear afraid even though I was more frightened than I had ever been. All I could think about was my son, and if anyone was getting hurt it was going to be me; he was not going to hurt my son. The dispatcher could hear everything, as I had the phone in my hand.

My husband was saying something about my son getting in his truck, and at that point, I had no idea what he was talking about, but I could see the rage in his eyes.

My husband turned around with the pickaxe in his hand and walked out the kitchen door and hit the plants on the porch outside the kitchen door with the pickaxe and then dropped it right there.

My son came back into the kitchen. He stood at the kitchen door shaking with the bat at his side. My husband had gotten in his car but got back out and told our son to come down there and fight like a man. I told my son to close the door and get in here. At the same time, two sheriff's vehicles pulled up. The deputies came into the kitchen and asked a few questions. I told them I already knew we are still legally married, and he can destroy anything at the marital home, but I just needed it documented.

The deputy said nothing and went back outside to the others. He came back in and told me my husband was being arrested. I started crying and begging the deputy not to arrest him. My son was right there just looking. He was in shock.

The deputy firmly told me to sit down and for my son to sit down. The deputy looked at me and said, "Mrs. ----, this is not O.K. Your son should not be afraid in his own home. These behaviors of your husband's have escalated, and it is not safe. He should not come to the door with a pickaxe and enter your home."

That is when my husband was taken to jail for the weekend and ended up in court on Monday morning for the initial charges. A restraining order was immediately put into effect which meant we could not see each other, nor could he see our minor son.

In July I received a message and agreed to meet with him even though we both knew there was a restraining order. He apologized once again and told me he was still my husband, and it did not matter what had happened. He told me he loved me, wanted me, and all those things I desperately wanted to be true. Once again, I succumbed, and the cycle continued. By August I sent a written request for the restraining order to be lifted so we could work on our marriage (he agreed to go to counseling again) and wanted him to be able to see our son. I was hopeful he would get help because of this incident. The court date for the hearing was set for September. He pleaded no contest as directed by his attorney. He was sentenced to three years' probation and ordered to attend domestic violence classes, which he did. The final summary from the domestic violence counselor was that he never owned what he did, and it was their recommendation that he continue in individual counseling because he blamed others for his own decisions and actions.

A week before the court hearing and sentencing I discovered another phone. I awoke one morning and had a nagging feeling. I must say that during this whole season the Holy Spirit would nudge me and lead me when I would listen. This particular morning I was led to a property we owned in a neighboring county. I could not understand why I was there. I looked around. We had a travel trailer parked there but it was locked. My husband had left a vehicle there and it was unlocked. I got in the driver's seat and opened the center console. I could not believe what I saw: another cell phone, with a prepaid card. This would be the fourth phone I found. In the console were a prescription bottle for men and another coinciding item. Once again, I was shocked, but this time composed. The phone was locked, and I could not see what was on it. I got a little angry with God at that point and I said, "You allow me to find this phone, but you will not let me unlock it to see what is on it?!" I think God protected me. He knows how much we can handle.

My hopes were shattered at this point, and I had no communication with my husband for at least six weeks. By mid-October, I agreed to see him. We began seeing one another again with hopes once again for reconciliation (at least on my part) even though the discovery of the fourth phone, prescription bottle for men, and other items were dismissed, denied, and deflected with no real discussion. He told me the pills were for me and the phone was never used. Somehow, I made excuses in my mind for it all in order to be with him and pursue reconciliation. There were never any apologies or repentance with evidence of change.

~

My husband spent Thanksgiving with us (all our children were there and some extended family). There seemed to be tension but relief on my children's part. The previous year was hard without their father present, but this year it was apparent that it was not that easy with him there either, as so much had transpired and nothing was ever discussed. Some of my children had also been recipients of derogatory texts and voicemails. Some of my children would call me or show me their phones and be so visibly upset at the words they heard or read from their father. I would continuously assure them that this is not the father they know, and something is wrong, and we will continue to pray. I would implore them to not receive those words, that God was not in them, and God desired the best for them and their father.

My husband was also invited to spend Christmas with us, and things seemed a little bit better. During all this time I was still not receiving any financial assistance from my husband, we were still living separately. I was paying bills with money from my job and the rents received from tenants in the rear of the property. I continued to make the college payments for my son who had received academic scholarships but there was still a balance to pay. I sold things out of the garage, I preached as a guest speaker and received offerings, I sold my wedding rings to a family member who would hold them for me until I could pay them back, and I also borrowed money from my mother for the first time in my life. Regardless, the tuition balance was paid every single time and the needs of my youngest son were met. My youngest son went to driver's education (paid for), got a beater car (paid for), grew six inches and three shoe sizes, and he had clothes and shoes that fit (paid for). God provided everything we needed right on time.

I continued to attend marital counseling alone. By the first of the year, I was continuing to see my husband, but we did not live together or see each other every day. What he did in the city where he now lived, how he spent his days and nights, I was never privy to. My life centered around my youngest son, the ministry, and my job. I had accountability in my life. I had friends that prayed for restoration, never spoke disparagingly about my husband, and who truly desired that we would reconcile. His acquaintances and few close "friends" did not have the same viewpoint. I dealt with one close friend who continued to send memes and videos to my husband's messenger account on social media that was connected to my email. Every derogatory meme and video would go to my email, and I could see what he would send to my husband and his comments. Even after I told this man I could see it and told my husband, it continued. I dealt with ridicule from his new best friends (who were all divorced except one). Of course, I realize, they only heard one side of the story and do not believe they knew of all the indiscretions, violence, and financial troubles.

One acquaintance stands out. He was a pastor at whose church I had ministered several times, and he thanked me for the "anointed word of God" and my ministry. He flipped like a light switch. He did not even meet my husband until after I ministered at his church, but this pastor became friends with my husband on social media and began to publicly post and comment negative things about me. It was to the extent that he commented on a live video feed while I was preaching; he called me Jezebel, laughed at me, and mocked me in the comments during my sermon. His comments were deleted by the pastor of the outreach, but after the event, someone told me what he had done, and I blocked him from my social media. He continued commenting on my husband's social media. He was certainly not rooting for our marriage to be reconciled, and to this day I cannot comprehend why he was just plain mean toward me. He was full of animosity, and he never once told me what problem he had with me. He went so far as to contact another pastor who had scheduled me to be part of a conference to tell him not to have me speak. I had never experienced this before in my life. It was an attack that I never understood, and it was so intentional. I had this person blocked and would never be able to defend myself even if I wanted to, yet he continuously spoke against me without justification or provocation. I had to choose forgiveness and pray for that pastor, but in no way did I have any further ministerial relationship with him.

Two years later I attended an inner-city church in Columbus that I have supported for many years. I did not know that that pastor was the guest speaker that evening. I arrived a little late and sat in the back; it was a full house. Many new Christians and others from recovery groups nearby were in attendance. My first reaction was to just leave, but I knew many people there and several waved to me as they saw me walk in, so I decided to stay. I did not want anything to affect their new walk with the Lord.

When the guest speaker saw me, he called me out and said, "Pastor Theresa is that you? Praise the Lord, good to see you." I could not believe it. I smiled and sat in my seat in the last row. He completed his sermon and began praying for people. I too prayed for those who were up front requesting prayer. I knew in my heart they were seeking God, developing a new relationship with their Lord and Savior, and I would not hinder that in any way.

As I was praying, once again the guest pastor called my name and said, "Pastor Theresa, come up here, I want to pray for you." I know now that I should have politely declined, but I accepted his invitation and went up front, even after his public derogatory remarks on social media about me. This was abusive behavior and I allowed him to bully me into coming up for prayer. The pastor laid his hand on my forehead and began praying. He was pushing me, and I know he wanted me to fall down but I did not. I have been in many Holy Spirit-filled services and have been blessed to see true moves of God, but I have also experienced the pushing and manipulation. I had my eyes closed and was praying at the same time, as I did not want any false prayers or curses laid on me. He stopped praying and my eyes were still closed when I felt a hit on my forehead from the palm of his hand that knocked my head back so hard my neck cracked. I opened my eyes, I was in pain and tears welled in my eyes, but I held my composure as well as I could. I turned around and walked back to my seat. One of my sons was there that night working in the sound booth. I could see him as I walked back to my seat and he could tell something was wrong. I tried to sit down but my neck hurt so bad. I gathered my things and left. I got to my car and put my hands on the back of my neck and began to pray. It hurt so terribly bad. That Pastor was a big guy, he hit my forehead full-on, and I had my eyes closed so I was not prepared for it. I prayed for God to touch my neck and heal me. I prayed all the way home. The next day it was still a little sore, but I knew God healed me.

I have never seen that pastor again, but I have heard he has continued to comment on social media negatively about me at times. Again, that Pastor has never come to me directly to tell me the problem he had with me. Once again, I chose forgiveness and prayed for that pastor.

> But I say unto you, love your enemies, bless them that curse you, do good to them that hate you, and pray for them which despitefully use you, and persecute you.
> – Matthew 5:44 KJV

Chapter 11

Because this revelation lamp now shines within you, nothing will be hidden from you – it will all be revealed. Every secret of the Kingdom will be unveiled and out in the open, made known by the revelation-light.

Luke 8:17 TPT

IT WAS THE BEGINNING OF the year, and we were heading into our second year of separation. We would continue to see each other but live separately. My husband occasionally came to the house and would spend the night, but I eventually stopped it because I thought it caused more issues for my youngest son. He questioned whether we were getting back together but then something would happen and destroy his hope. During one of those evenings, my husband left his phone unlocked and on the table. I picked it up and once again saw more porn on his phone. This time it included Craigslist "Casual Encounters" sites. It seemed this just continued to progress.

Around this time, I was informed by a former tenant's daughter that her mother had filed a police report against my husband before our separation. I went online and read the report. It stated that she was being evicted for refusing to go out to dinner with him. I contacted the woman and spoke with her. I flat-out asked her if she had sex with my husband. She would not answer directly. She told me he came to her work forty minutes away to pick up rent and that he wanted her to go out for drinks, but she had to work. She said that he came over often while she was "sick." I was also told how he offered other ways for her to pay rent. I really did not know what to believe at that point but considering his internet history and all the rumors I had heard in the community, nothing surprised me at all. This woman knew a lot about my husband. I remembered that when they had first moved in he took pictures of her and her teenage daughter and showed them to me, saying he thought the daughter looked like our foster daughter. I asked him why he took pictures of a new tenant (whom I could see was quite attractive), but he deflected by saying it was no big deal and asked me, "What is your problem?"

By the end of January, a note was taped to my door (at the marital home) stating that he was turning off the electricity that was still in his name. My youngest son saw the note and would call me from school to ask if the electricity was still on. I assured him that if his father followed through with it, I would have the electricity turned back on and put in my name. Well, the electricity was turned off and I had the electric company put it in my name after paying a $600 deposit. The electricity bills for the large home were very high and included the power for the tenants who lived in the unit at the rear of the property. They had started paying my husband the rent again, so I informed them that if they did not pay the rent to me, they would have to move because I could not pay the electricity bill without their rent payments. They obliged and understood. I also had to put the gas in my name which cost another considerable amount for the deposit.

Dropping the initial legal separation agreement and not receiving any support for nearly a year was difficult, to say the least. I held on to hope but there were times he sent such vulgar, nasty, unkind texts and voicemails it began to take a toll. I would repeatedly choose forgiveness. I continued the cycle of not seeing or speaking to him for weeks at a time, only to be sweet-talked into seeing him, being intimate, and then once again discarded. Most upsetting was hearing about the continued texts and voicemails my children would get. They often blocked him as well. He truly was not the man I used to know. He was unrecognizable and his behaviors were unpredictable.

I chose forgiveness continuously, but what I failed to recognize is that forgiveness is not absent of consequences. Forgiveness means giving up my desire for vengeance and giving it to God, the God of justice. I ignored the fact that trust was broken, and continued to be broken. Forgiveness does not give back trust without evidence of change and accountability. Forgiveness is between me and God—ensuring my heart is right, and that I do not desire vengeance or retaliation. Restored trust and reconciliation could only happen if there was the fruit of true repentance (transformed behaviors, actions, and turning away from the sin). There would need to be the fruit of repentance, which is lasting, not just a few days or weeks.

I had to accept that my husband's continued behavior had no evidence of repentance or true desire to restore our marriage. Blatant lies, half-truths, unwillingness to fully disclose all the hidden secrets and sin—it was all lying and emotionally abusive behavior. I made excuses continuously and reasoned in my mind and soul that ignoring the behavior was required of me as a Christian woman, wife, and mother.

I have learned by reading many books, studies, and statistics by wise Christian men and women that my experience was not isolated and is more prevalent than the Christian community wants to acknowledge. I wanted reconciliation so badly that I was willing to forgo true repentance, accountability, and the consequences of the broken covenant to just get to forgiveness and healing. What I learned is that there cannot be healing without repentance, full disclosure, and acknowledgment of the consequences of the choices that were made, which included betrayal and infidelity. I chose forgiveness, but trust could never be rebuilt without repentance and my husband taking ownership of his role in breaking the covenant of marriage, not to mention him needing to have a true desire to rebuild. God is all about restoration and reconciliation where true humility and full surrender are present to allow Father God to operate and heal the damage. In a marriage, both husband and wife must desire reunification and be willing to do whatever it takes.

The behaviors that were present with my spouse were consistent with what a psychologist would term narcissism. The cycle of behaviors that lured me in, only to be repeatedly discarded and my hopes shattered was evidence of such. I want to be very clear about this: I was only treated kindly during the years of separation when he wanted sex. It would be no more than three days—often as soon as the next evening—that he would be out with his friends, sending me hateful texts and/or voicemails telling me what a horrible woman I was, how I should be ashamed, how no one would ever want me, and how I would be nothing without him. This behavior is certainly not the biblical vision of what a husband should be! I continued to put on masks for a long time and remained stoic. What I learned and received is that God does not expect us to remain stoic and put our masks back on to avoid embarrassing God with our suffering or the fact, in my case, that my marriage had been broken. We are not better Christians when we call the hardest parts of life "good." We can learn to call God good in those hard parts and lament at the same time. We know God will be with us, we belong to Him, and He is a good, good Father. I truly learned to give God my weakness and receive His strength.

Chapter 12

Being confident of this very thing, that he which hath begun a good work in you will perform it until the day of Jesus Christ.

Philippians 1:6 KJV

We had been saved thirty-three years before our separation—radically saved on a Friday night at an inner-city church at 9:00 PM. The service was already over, and the only people left in the church were the pastor and three ladies who were prayer warriors. The minister, who my boyfriend at the time worked with, had been telling us about Jesus and His love and His forgiveness, and this man not only talked the talk but walked the walk. There were times I would pick up my boyfriend of two years from work (usually around nine at night) and this minister somehow needed a ride home. There would be alcohol bottles, cigarettes, and even pot odors in the vehicle and the minister would not say a thing about it. He would just talk about the goodness of God and our need for a savior. He began planting seeds, and before you knew it my boyfriend and I were not doing any of the same things anymore. No more partying, no more fooling around, nothing.

This led right up to Friday night when we wanted to be baptized. The minister took us to his church, we repented, were baptized in water, and formally received Jesus as our Lord and Savior. My boyfriend wanted to be filled with the Holy Spirit and the pastor instructed him to pray for me. He knelt in front of me and prayed and began to speak in tongues. I had never experienced that before. I knew it was God. I believed it and wanted it, too. About a week later, I was filled with the Holy Spirit. We were saved and at that point already engaged. My family did not respond well to my newfound faith or the engagement. We were planning to get married the following fall (this was January 1983) but knew we did not want to wait. During this time, I was living with the minister and his family who first introduced us to Jesus. My boyfriend had a little house that was barely livable and he was renovating it. We were married a few weeks later and I moved into his home. We worked on it, made it a home, and served God. We became part of the new ministry the pastor started in the inner city. We attended every Bible study, every church service, and would travel with the minister wherever he would go to be a guest speaker. We learned so much in the Word of God. We grew leaps and bounds and experienced the moving of the Holy Spirit in such tangible ways. Our faith grew and we learned to tithe and give abundantly, even when we only brought home $200 a week. God provided for us. We were sold out for the Lord.

I share this little glimpse to show our foundation was on the rock - Jesus. We started on solid ground. I loved my husband and I believe he loved me. We had our first child, a daughter, a year and ten months after we were married. We moved from that first little home and purchased another where we had a pony and puppies. We walked out our Christian faith in action and not just words. We were part of outreaches and gave more than a tithe of our income. We loved God and all that He had done in our lives. We were radically saved.

My husband began studying, preaching, and teaching early on. I was quiet and did not speak publicly at all. I attended the Bible study classes and the ministerial classes, but I did not speak in public. I supported my husband. He became quite an anointed and powerful preacher. Our family grew over the years through adoption and foster parenting, as well as giving birth to more children. I had always wanted a big family and God blessed me with just that.

After many years of training, sitting in classes, and assisting my husband, God began opening doors for me to preach and teach. I was also ordained and began walking in ministry alongside my husband. We ministered throughout Ohio, went on mission trips overseas, and traveled out of state to hold meetings while still being active in our local church. We moved out of the city to a small town where we became members of the Foursquare Church for over a decade. During that time, we started a youth center for at-risk youth that was open daily. This would become a stressful time, and yet the most rewarding time in our lives. After eight years of running the youth center, I could no longer do it with a preschooler and baby at home, along with my teenage children, so we sold the building.

By this time my husband had begun purchasing some investment property for our future retirement. I continued to stay home with our children, and we were still foster parents, so we always had children in the home. We ended up refurbishing a large old home and moving there. I was not personally excited about the move but made it a home. More rental property was acquired and a new lifestyle began. We still attended church, but my husband was preaching less and I was preaching more as doors were opened. As I said before, you can look back and see the slow fade, but while it is happening you do not notice it as clearly.

Three years before our initial separation we began the ministry where we were co-pastors. I completed all the paperwork to register the non-profit and we began holding evening services, and then Sunday afternoon services. God moved and lives were touched, yet we were having relationship issues from the beginning. When we were separated and my husband stopped coming to the ministry, the only thing I knew for sure was that God told me to "preach through the pain," and that is what I did. The ministry continued with the help of godly assistant ministers and all the needs were met. God always showed up in our meetings and I am forever grateful to have been part of that ministry. Lives were transformed through the healing of souls and bodies, needs were met, and most of all Jesus was lifted up and many were drawn to Him. To God be the glory!

Chapter 13

I am convinced that my God will fully satisfy every need you have, for I have seen the abundant riches of glory revealed to me through Jesus Christ! And God our Father will receive all the glory and the honor throughout the eternity of eternities! Amen!

Philippians 4:19-20 TPT

By the spring of the second year of our separation—and one year since I dropped the initial legal separation filing—I continued to preach and teach. I was working a job and preparing to go on a mission trip to Sri Lanka. I had been invited to be part of a team, and what a team it was! It was a privilege and an experience in God I will never forget. God miraculously provided all the means for me to go, but it was not without its challenges. My husband laughed and mocked me for going to Sri Lanka. Initially, I was not going to accept the invitation because I thought it was not possible—I had no funds. One of my sons reminded me that he had been to church many times when words were given to me that I would be traveling to other nations, and he encouraged me to accept the invitation. I did and trusted God for provision and every part of the trip was paid for by so many unexpected people and circumstances. One contributor was an old acquaintance from high school. We had become friends on social media, and she was watching some of my ministry events. She contacted me and asked to meet for dinner. While at dinner she handed me money and said that God told her to give it to me for my trip. I was overwhelmed by her generosity and the goodness of God the Father. He has *always* provided for me!

This was the second mission trip I went on while separated from my husband. The previous year I had returned to Haiti, and once again God opened that door and provided the resources. It was an amazing thing to be going through such a difficult season in my personal life, but to go and serve others. Doing so brought healing to my heart. It was also a reminder that God fulfills his promises, as I knew through prayer and prophetic words that I would be traveling and ministering in other nations. God's timing is always perfect even when we don't understand how it could be. Going on these God-ordained trips to serve ministered to me and brought healing to my broken heart and strengthened my spirit.

My husband and I were not seeing one another regularly, but I was still praying and believing God to restore our marriage. I did not date, develop friendships with men, or "put myself out there." In my heart and mind, I was still married. I had gone over a year without any support, and it was becoming more and more difficult to make ends meet. I had a son in college and a son in high school, and I was the sole caregiver. My husband continued to live in Columbus, collect the rents (by this time I was not involved at all, not even doing paperwork), had his paycheck, and did not pay support of any kind. I had no choice but to refile for legal separation and request spousal support due to the instability of my housing and the need for funds for my sons' necessities and tuition. My husband never owned up to his infidelity and betrayal, and he continued his lifestyle as a single man without any accountability. I contacted my attorney and had him refile for legal separation. I told my husband I was refiling, but I do not think he believed me.

While I was in Sri Lanka, I received text messages from my husband, because he received his copy of the filing while I was away. To say he was angry is an understatement. I had to block his number again. When I got back from the trip there was no communication for a while. I continued my life as a mother, clerk, and minister. He stopped over occasionally, and I would agree to have dinner with him, but it would always turn volatile with berating remarks.

In the summer of this second year of separation, after my trip to Sri Lanka, my husband came to the home. I was upstairs getting changed, my collegiate son was home in his room, and my youngest son was outside with his friend. My husband came into the home uninvited and unbeknownst to me. I heard a knock on my bedroom door, and I thought it was one of my sons. I said I would be out in a minute, but my doorknob started to turn. I locked it immediately. I had an extra lock put on my door months prior, as my husband had once come into the home early in the morning and came into my room and refused to leave (I got out safely). I could hear that it was my husband on the other side of the door. I got dressed quickly and went downstairs. My sons looked shocked because they had not seen their dad in a while, and the fact that he just walked in and came upstairs was unsettling. He was outside yelling, stopped in the driveway and peed in the middle of the driveway, then walked to his new vehicle. He got back out of his car and walked over to the stone wall along the driveway and began pushing on it. He knocked over a six-foot section of a four-foot wall. My youngest son started to yell at his dad and ran after him as he got back in his car. I had to yell at my son to get back. Once again, I had to call the sheriff to file a report. He was charged a few weeks later with a felony for coming into the house without permission. I called the sheriff's department because I could not understand why he was charged with a felony—I had only reported the incident because of damage. They informed me that we are separated, and he cannot enter the home without being invited. He had to go to court for his actions and deal with the consequences. I wrote a letter to the court to ask for leniency. Although I did not want him charged with a felony, it did not take away my concern over his erratic and unpredictable behaviors. I always kept my doors locked from then on. I had my concealed carry license and always carried my gun. I became very aware of my surroundings. After that incident we did not see one another for weeks on end. There would be small communications but nothing face-to-face, and I was no longer taking the bait for dinner that led to sex.

We had our first court date for the new filing and immediately the judge ordered that all rental property be given to a receivership as my husband had not been making the mortgage payments or property tax payments for two months but was collecting rents. This action from the judge was a costly one, but it was the consequence of my husband's actions. This decision meant all rents were handled by the receivership, all maintenance, and all bills. My husband was livid. The receivership was an attorney's office so their fees were exorbitant. The consequence of intentionally not paying mortgages and collecting rents was thousands of dollars. My husband was also ordered to begin immediately paying support again, and it was back-dated to the day of refiling. This led to more berating, disparaging texts and voicemails, so the need to block him again was inevitable. I found myself still holding on to God, believing for a full turnaround.

I believe God answers prayers and I believed it was God's will that our marriage be restored. I also now recognize that without repentance, healing could not happen. The porn viewing had escalated and was sought after through Facebook, Pinterest, Tumbler, Craigslist ... I never knew how readily available porn was. My spouse still had the second phone at his condo, and still denied it all. He would say, "Just because it is on my phone doesn't make it true." The level of deception was great and there was no remorse for any of it. I had to grasp that pornography had corrupted my husband's view of sex, women, and personal relationships. Porn is like poison, and every time a person clicks on a porn site the corruption of the heart is deepened. Porn creates a barrier between the person viewing it and their loved ones. Porn causes the viewer to shy away from meaningful conversations since they have a secret fantasy life going on inside that causes a gap from reality. The important things in life lose their appeal next to porn, and that includes their spouse and family.

I do not believe my husband intended that to happen, it is just a consequence of the addiction or stronghold to porn. I believe there becomes a disconnect, and the lack of genuine affection for spouse and family is a residual effect. All I could do was pray and when new revelations came out, I would have to choose again to forgive. Forgiveness is for us, not the other party. Forgiveness protects our hearts from bitterness. Forgiveness vacillates. You will have good days and bad days, but I had to choose forgiveness and stay the course. Forgiveness keeps us free whether we ever get an apology or not. I chose forgiveness 24/7.

Chapter 14

I know you're able and I know you can
Save through the fire with Your mighty hand
But even if You don't
My hope is You alone
I know the sorrow, and I know the hurt
Would all go away if You'd just say the word
But even if You don't
My hope is You alone

"Even If" lyrics by Mercy Me

In October, just a couple months after the court date for the second legal separation, I received a call from my husband. He was distraught, crying, and said he needed to go to the emergency room. He had just left his physical from work and his blood sugar was dangerously high. He asked me to take him. I did. He was brought into the ER and spent about eight hours there. He was given insulin and was told to go to the doctor first thing Monday morning (this was a Friday). He was told not to be alone for the weekend. I brought him home with me to the marital home. I informed our son he would be staying with us until he was seen by the doctor. I was part of a DivorceCare group on Sunday evenings (I would recommend this group to anyone going through separation or divorce) and left to attend my meeting for a couple hours. During that time my husband left to meet his friends. The next day I took him to the doctor where it was discovered that his health situation was extremely serious. He was prescribed medications and had many appointments lined up. He came back to the home, and I had to go to work for a few hours. I received a call from him right when I was clocking out and I could tell he was in distress. He was very sick. I rushed home, put him in the car, and took him to the hospital. He was in a great deal of pain. We drove fifteen minutes to the hospital. I had to pull over so he could vomit. We arrived at the ER and he was brought back to a room. His blood sugar level was high again, and he had severe abdominal pain. He was admitted to the hospital within hours of arriving at the ER. He was taken for X-rays, given an insulin adjustment, and hooked up to many machines. It was discovered that he had kidney stones. The hope was that they would pass on their own, but they did not.

He was in the hospital for a couple of days after they placed a stent to help with the stones in his bladder. I stayed with him and never went home. I called my job and told them I had a family medical emergency and would not be back until further notice. I needed that income, but I knew I was to stay with my husband. My daughter bought me clothes and some food and watched over her youngest brother who was in high school. After two days he was still in serious pain and carrying a temperature, and it was determined that surgery was needed to insert a stent to drain his kidney infection which was a life-threatening issue. We were hopeful that the surgery would resolve everything.

From the moment he was admitted to the hospital I placed him on the prayer list at church. Many were praying for the healing of his body as well as praying for his spirit man. To be honest, the whole family believed this would be used for the glory of God and the turnaround would happen. He would be healed, repentance would happen, and our marriage would be restored. While we were waiting for him to be released I stayed in the room with him and never left the hospital. All our children visited when able and allowed. He appeared to be doing much better. His blood sugar was remaining stable since it was being diligently monitored and managed at the hospital. The doctors diagnosed him with diabetes and emphasized to us how serious it was and the need to control it and make lifestyle changes. There was no arguing with that. My husband had an unhealthy weight, and his job did not help with getting into shape. We knew it would take a true lifestyle change, and I was willing to help and support him to make those changes.

Within two days of the surgery his health declined again. He started running a fever that they could not keep down. He began becoming delirious. He was incoherent most of the time. I demanded answers and requested the doctor to come in. My two youngest sons were there that day and could see their father was not in a good state. I had been up all night with him, as he would be calling out and thrashing in the bed. I would sing to him spiritual songs and worship songs and he would calm down and be at peace. While my sons were there, they also saw him thrashing and visibly uncomfortable. Once again, I would softly sing while gently rubbing his head and arms. We prayed and laid hands on him. We believed God would heal him. We believed this was the turnaround.

The doctor finally arrived and saw the severity of what was happening. He determined that my husband was in severe sepsis and had to be transferred to another hospital. Once again, prayer warriors were notified. I called all the children to notify them. I had to gather all our things as by that time we had been in the hospital for about six days.

He was transported by ambulance and I drove separately. He was brought up to a normal inpatient floor, and I must acknowledge the nurse on duty was instrumental in saving his life. She immediately said, "He should not be here! He needs to be brought to the ICU immediately!" He was brought to the ICU where he remained for three nights. They were three nights of intense prayer and standing in faith that he would survive and be healed and restored. I slept in a chair in the ICU. I never left the hospital. My daughter made sure I had food and whatever else I needed.

He was released from the ICU into a step-down room and then to another room. There were many doctors in and out, many who were specialists. He had sustained kidney damage and only time would tell if it was permanent or if it would heal. There was also heart damage, as his heart was only operating at 50% and once again time would tell if it would heal. There was a whole new daily routine at the hospital that would be continued after he was released. It involved testing blood sugar many times a day, insulin shots, and changing the urine bag. I took notes and listened to instructions. There were a few days when my husband needed help and needed to be cleaned from bodily functions. I made sure his dignity was intact and I cleaned him. I cleaned up messes so the nurses would not have to, but more to protect him and his dignity. I am grateful to have been there and able to do it. Again, I genuinely believed this was going to be a new beginning, a beginning of restoration.

He was released from the hospital and came home with me. The new normal was testing his blood sugar, insulin shots, changing bags every three hours, physical therapy, and many doctor's appointments, and making sure his diet was conducive to getting healthy. I would set my alarm in the night to change the bag and keep the insulin schedule. I believed he would not have to be on insulin once the weight came off and his body healed. It truly would require a lifestyle change. During this time, we were still dealing with our separation court dates as well as his court dates for charges of trespassing. I contacted my attorney to drop the separation immediately due to all he had been through physically and the fact that he was now living with me and I was caring for him. I told my attorney we were reuniting, and he has changed. My attorney said he would draw up documents, but since it is at this stage in the separation it will take time to submit. He reminded me that if I dropped the separation again, it would also stop my support. I assured my attorney once again that I understood but believed we were reuniting, and it was going to be alright.

My husband was off work and there was no income. I helped him apply for temporary disability through his job and submitted all the paperwork. There were bills as well as his pending court case. I wrote a letter to the court asking them to reconsider the charges against him, stating that he had changed, and this action was not the man he always was. I pleaded in my letter to drop the case so he could heal and be restored with his family. Once again, I was writing a letter to the court and making excuses, but I truly believed this was our new beginning, our second chance, our redemption story.

My husband began discussing retirement and what that would look like. We discussed selling our marital home, selling some of the rentals, and downsizing to live with less stress and responsibility. Considering he came close to death, you would think this would be a no-brainer. He began getting stronger and we were even able to go out to dinner for his birthday for a couple of hours with our children. He agreed to get counseling and we found a local marriage counselor to see, as I had stopped seeing my counselor after two and a half years (I am forever grateful for the wisdom and anointing of my counselor). We attended a couple of sessions with this new counselor, but my husband was very aloof about it. I reasoned it was because he was still recovering from being so ill and it would take time.

I continued to care for him. He would not give himself the insulin, so I had to give it to him four times a day, testing his blood sugar before and after meals. He was still doing physical therapy but began driving himself to check on rentals and such against my wishes. One evening he had gone to bed early but came back downstairs shortly after, panicking about there being blood present. We headed to the emergency room. While we were there, he left his phone in the car. He insisted I get it for him when he learned he was going to be kept overnight. When I went down to get it, I looked at it. I had no time to check his phone while he had been at home with me, so this was the first time I looked at his search history. Once again, pornography was on the phone. This time I was upset but composed. I brought the phone to him and said I would see him in the morning. He was released quickly, as there was nothing seriously wrong. He was simply still in recovery. I brought him back home and we were to go to marital counseling again the following day. He told me he was not going. I had not yet disclosed to him that I saw what was on his phone and was waiting to bring it up in counseling so we would have someone to guide us through dealing with this continued issue and bondage.

When he refused to go to counseling, I became angry. I flipped out and I yelled at him and said I saw his phone and what was on it. I asked him how he could continue looking at porn. I sat there and looked at him and told him, "I was willing to fight with you and fight for you to be delivered from this addiction, this bondage but you do not want to." I was crying, I was yelling, and I was done. He grabbed his phone and left. I had to go to the radio station for my ministry program.

When I returned, he was back. There was a flip phone sitting on the table next to him. I picked up the phone and laughed. I yelled at him, thinking in my mind, *Are you serious, you went out now and bought a flip phone, but you will not talk to me, you never acknowledge any of it, tell the truth or even apologize. How many phones is this?* I picked up the phone and threw it across the room.

He was upset, yelling, and telling me he got that phone so he would not have Internet on his phone. Honestly, for a minute I felt bad, but then I knew it was not the truth. He got up angrily after I did not respond to that statement and said, "You broke my phone, and I am calling the police." And he did. I told him he needed to leave. I gathered up his medications along with the instructions before the police showed up.

The police arrived and I told them I asked him to leave. At that point, my husband was refusing to leave. The police told me since he had been staying a few weeks there was nothing they could do. It was a civil matter and they left. Within an hour my husband decided to go ahead and leave. He was not going to take his medication, so I carried it out and put it into his car on the passenger seat. When I opened the door to put the tub of medicines and insulin in, there was his old smartphone plugged in to the car. He hadn't traded it in for a flip phone, he just got a flip phone to make it look like he was going to not have a smartphone. He still had his phone, but the new one was going to be cover for his continued sin.

He went back to his condominium. I struggled with guilt since I had taken care of him throughout his major illness where he almost died. I had taken him home and cared for him, made sure he took his meds, checked his glucose, and gave him his insulin. Would he do what he was supposed to do? He had already said he was not going to take the insulin. Would he eat properly and stop drinking alcohol? I still loved and cared for him, but I knew he made his choices, and I could not force him to choose God, choose me, or choose his family. My attorney had not filed the dismissal for separation and the criminal case was still lingering against my husband. The criminal case was eventually dismissed but our separation hearings continued. After being at the hospital for close to two weeks with my husband, praying for his healing, seeing God preserve his life, bringing him home to recuperate, and then once again seeing he chose to continue in porn viewing, escort sites, dating sites, back page, Craigslist hookup sites, and friendships that never encouraged him to fight for his marriage or be delivered, I became disillusioned.

I know I am not the only one who has experienced these things, and many have experienced far worse. One thing I do know is that women who are wounded by betrayal, infidelity and toxic relationships while being in the faith community or church world can lose faith. You begin to wonder how a loving God could allow so much hurt. When "Christians" hurt us, whether at home, in our family, or at church it creates a soundtrack in our minds that spits out lies about who we are, how we are to act and what we are worth.

I fought the lies of the enemy going on three years by this point. I dealt with harsh words from my husband spoken to me, texted to me, or left on voicemails. I had to deal with other Christians who thought I was to accept the betrayal, that porn is "no big deal," and stay quiet, and the other Christians who thought I should have left a long time ago and kick him to the curb. It was a struggle that, to the Christian world I lived in, my choosing to separate made me the one who had broken the covenant. You see, to some it does not matter if he broke vows and continued in the betrayal and infidelity—as a wife you are to stay. Then I had to deal with the feeling that, because I did not continue to stay and accept the continued betrayal and breaking of vows, I had betrayed God because God hates divorce. The truth was I did not want divorce, which is why I filed only for separation. I wanted restoration and reconciliation, but it became clear that was not going to happen. Every individual has a will to choose what they want. My former husband never chose me.

A shift had been taking place. I realized I was not the same person I used to be. I could not tolerate the things I used to. I was speaking truth about the bondage and about the betrayal, and it was not an argument anymore. I realized and accepted that God did not want me to accept the cruelty, the betrayal, or the moral compromise (sin). I (none of us) can make excuses and call good, evil and evil, good. God loves me, He really does. God's heart breaks when our hearts break. God does not want us to pretend everything is good when it is not. But we can always say, "God you are good, always." God was and continues to be faithful to me.

The next month was once again Christmas. This would be the third Christmas of being separated. I prepared for the holidays and continued our family traditions. It seemed that I thought, by making everything "normal," it would somehow ease the pain for my children. I know it did not. Everything in me wanted my children not to hurt or be affected by their parents' marriage failing. I had no control over the consequences or the pain that was and continues to be felt. I could only grieve with them and for them. I know they blamed me many times for filing for separation, but I also know they never knew the full spectrum of what was happening. Even in authoring this book, I am being protective of how much I reveal to protect my children. There is much that will continue to be private, but I honestly believe sharing part of my journey and the devastation of a failed Christian marriage, and the precursors that led to the separation and in the end, divorce, need to be exposed within the Christian community. No one talks about this. No one shares the fact that the same temptations in "the world" are in "the church," and although we as Spirit-filled Christians are to resist the temptations, the reality is that many succumb and in turn are overtaken. Porn is an addictive tool used by the enemy, and it has destroyed individuals, marriages, families, churches, and ministries.

I let my son tell his father he was welcome to join us for Christmas Eve and Christmas Day. He did attend and stayed all night. Things went well without incident. All our children were there Christmas morning, and it was good for them that both their parents were present. I know it brought hope that reconciliation would come. I knew within me that unless inward transformation was allowed to take place, it would not happen. I once again thought being intimate would cause change and once again it did not. He left on Christmas Day in the early afternoon. I later learned through a contractor who worked for my husband's brother that my husband told his brother, "Christmas was horrible and all hell broke loose."

The only reason I heard this was that the contractor's wife called (they both attended my ministry) and asked if I was O.K. I was shocked to hear that was what my husband told his brother since this final Christmas celebration with us all present went very well. I did ask my husband why he said that and he denied it. I dropped it. By New Year's Eve I agreed to have dinner with him. This dinner was not easy. There was a disconnect. He did come back to the home and stay but I had to work the next day at 6 A.M. I said goodbye that morning and headed to work.

At 10 A.M. I had a break. I looked at my phone and had a voicemail from my husband. The voicemail said, "If you do not drop the separation, I am filing for divorce." I had to complete my shift while grieving. I knew I could not drop the separation because nothing had changed. In fact, things were worse and there had never been a desire to work on the marriage, fight for our marriage, fight against the addiction, forsake all others, and allow healing that only God could bring to our relationship. I chose forgiveness, but forgiveness does not automatically mean trust is restored. Repentance never happened and there was no fruit of repentance. My heart grieved but I trusted God.

By mid-January I received my notice of his counter for divorce, which meant he had already countered for divorce when we met on New Year's Eve, when I once again was intimate with him (stupid, I know). He knew he was divorcing me. He had a new attorney (his third). By this point the legalities with all the paperwork had already been done, as some of the legalities are the same for legal separation. This new attorney was a bit late to this party but was from a prestigious law firm that cost thousands of dollars. We had to attend interrogations where each attorney asked the other party questions which would be recorded. Some of the questions were quite frankly silly and not relevant. The original complaint for separation stated infidelity and cruelty yet included my desire for reconciliation. The counter for divorce was "irreconcilable differences." There was no biblical basis for my husband suing me for divorce. I had biblical grounds, yet believed God was able to restore our marriage and heal our relationship and that is why I still held on for over three years and only filed for separation.

During the interrogation, my husband was asked about his porn use. His answer, which was recorded, was, "So what. Big deal. It's not against the law." There was no remorse. No sorry. No sadness. I got up from the table and told my attorney, I am not doing this (as my husband's words were crushing, as if I was hit straight on in my gut) and my attorney stopped his questioning. Although my husband's response was short, no one in that room knew the length of time it had been going on, the residual effects of the porn, the progression of the porn and how it led to so much more. Possibly everyone in that room believed what he said was true, that porn is no big deal. I will tell you that porn is a life altering habit and its insidious effects will change a person and take the person farther than they ever imagined they would go. After the interrogations were done and we were getting ready to leave I had another emotional response to the whole experience.

I looked at his new attorney, who happened to be wearing a blouse that opened and showed cleavage, and said to her, "You might want to be careful with your blouse, he likes that." I then began to say to my soon-to-be-former husband, "How much porn? It's O.K. now, and not against the law?"

My attorney interrupted and told me to stop and that we needed to leave. It was an emotional, wrong response to have, and the Holy Spirit was not leading me to act that way. My self-control had improved so much by that point, but it quickly reverted to lashing out that day and it is not a moment I am proud of.

We continued to have meetings with attorneys to try to come to an agreement. At first, I wanted to stay in the home for my son's sake, but after so much going back and forth and knowing my husband wanted all his properties, including the marital home, I was at peace offering to move and reaching a tentative agreement. I was no longer lashing out and had a renewed mind to remain under the divine influence of the Holy Spirit. Many people told me 50% is yours, you are entitled, etc. I prayed about it all and I knew peace is priceless. I chose peace.

Chapter 15

Woe to those who call evil good and good evil, who put darkness for light and light for darkness, who put bitter for sweet and sweet for bitter.

Isaiah 5:20 KJV

IF YOU HAD MET ME or ran into me during the three and a half years of my separation, I would smile and laugh at a joke, and you would never know my heart was broken into a million shattered pieces. You would never know I was so filled with fear that I constantly quoted scriptures to myself, and that I wondered at 52, 53, 54, 55 years old if I am worth much. I'm now closer to 60 than 50 and have finally accepted that my former husband's infidelity and choice to use porn was not my fault. I am not to blame for not looking like the images of the other women. I have become confident in my identity in Jesus Christ. There are times I am triggered by porn-related things that are out of my control, like when I went to an auto repair shop and they told me to come back to the garage to show me an issue with my wheel, and there in plain view was a pornographic calendar. I told the man to put my wheel back on and that I was leaving, and that I did not appreciate having to see porn and how unprofessional that was. I was short with the mechanic and not nice about it, but I realized how the residual effects of the betrayal impacted me. Sometimes, fully trusting again seems impossible. With the statistics of porn viewing and the progression of continued use, no one is exempt.

Pornography in all forms is an epidemic in our society. There is a relatively new organization called Fight the New Drug. How appropriate to use that term. In my research to find out why this was such an issue, I discovered the scientific effects on a person's brain from continued viewing of porn. The damage to the brain is like that of a heroin addict. Truly, porn is "the new drug," but in actuality it is not new and has been around a long time. The difference today is it is right at your fingertips, and it will take submitting to God in order for the devil to flee from you. It will take full surrender to the Holy Spirit, it will take hypervigilance to resist the temptation, and it will take the church world to acknowledge its profound effects on lives, families, and relationships to become a catalyst for change.

Pornography is a secret addiction and stronghold even in the church. The statistics are staggering. The aftermath has reached far into the destruction of marriage, families, and communities. It changes the mindsets of all those involved and opens the door to more perversion and other demonic influences. Listen, Jesus is still the answer! Jesus still delivers captives! The body of Christ needs to be praying. We cannot be surprised when things of this world are accomplished in our brethren. Awake and arise, church! Be zealous to repent! Jesus did not come to fix the symptoms; He came to break the cycle.

We need to understand that people just do not "fall into sin." Leaders, called ministers, and anointed men and women don't wake up one day and say, "I want to destroy my ministry, my family, and my marriage." The enemy schemes and comes subtly. Rebellion is one of the favorite gateways for a Jezebel spirit (and that is not gender-specific as it's used so often in the church world). A Jezebel spirit comes with a haughty attitude and refusal of wise counsel.

We need to understand that pornography exploits, degrades, humiliates, abuses, and objectifies women. Most of the women in those pictures or videos are not willing participants. Pornography viewing supports human trafficking. We need to understand that pornography hurts men and takes from their potential and value. Pornography viewing by men will cause them insecurity, as they do not measure up to the standard of appearance or performance. Porn viewing by men often leaves them depressed and lonely, as it is done in secret and in turn they are lying about their actions. Porn is full of lies directed at men that often cause their sense of "what it means to be a man" to be distorted. As porn reduces women to objects for men's pleasure, porn reduces men to instruments of power and domination instead of true leaders in the biblical vision of manhood.

~

The statistics reveal that the increase in the amount and the reach of pornography cannot be ignored. It does not just affect men but also women, teens, and children (who are caught in the web of porn) at alarming rates. Many Christians think that the Church is immune, as no way would godly folk be viewing porn. The truth is that porn has invaded the church. The following statistics are from December 2020 by Kingdom Works Studios, The Conquer Series:

- Over forty million Americans are regular visitors to porn sites.
- There are forty-two million porn websites.
- The porn industry's annual revenue is more than the NFL, NBA, and MLB combined. Also, more than CBS, NBC, and ABC combined.
- 47% of families in the US reported that pornography is a problem in their homes. Pornography use increases the marital infidelity rate by more than 300%.

- Eleven is the average age that a child is first exposed to porn, and 94% of children will see it by age fourteen.
- 56% of American divorces involve one party having an "obsessive interest" in pornographic websites.
- 70% of Christian youth pastors report that they have had at least one teen come to them for help in dealing with pornography in the last year.
- 68% of church-going men and over 50% of pastors view porn on a regular basis. Of young Christian adults eighteen to twenty-four years old, 76% actively search for porn.
- 59% of pastors said that married men seek help for porn use.
- 33% of women aged twenty-five and under search for porn at least once per month.
- Only 13% of self-identified Christian women say they never watch porn; 87% of Christian women have watched porn.
- 55% of married men and 25% of married women say they watch porn at least once a month.
- 57% of pastors say porn addiction is the most damaging issue in their congregation. 69 % say porn has adversely impacted the church.

It's overwhelming to see these stats and realize the effects on our society. This amount of consumption, along with the church's silence around the topic of sexuality, has distorted the sexual development of millions of young men and women who now have grown up in a pornified society. The consequences are detrimental as we now see them coming to the surface, as many millennials begin to marry and attempt to attain healthy marital relationships while relying on the false reality of what they viewed in pornography. The church must be willing to fight against it, expose it, and stand up to acknowledge there is a problem. You cannot treat a disease until you know it is there. We must realize that if left unchecked and ignored, this disease will grow.

Not only is porn more accessible in the digital context, but unsolicited porn has increased substantially on the Internet. The usage among young women has grown significantly when it was once thought it was a man's domain. The acceptance of porn as "no big deal" has entered the church. Many young adults think not recycling is worse than viewing porn. The beautiful God-given gift of sex within the marriage covenant is being so distorted by the fake images being viewed. Some young Christians even compromise their thought process about it by thinking it is O.K. to look at porn if you are not actually having sex before marriage. These are all lies fed to those viewing.

The attire that young women wear has morphed into this hypersexual look. I am not a prude by any means, and I do not buy into the religious spirit that women must wear long dresses, avoid makeup, and keep their hair in a bun. I like to dress in current styles, look feminine, and wear makeup. But I am talking about shorts so short you might as well wear your underwear in public. Exposing all body parts, wearing items that advertise the name of pornography producers, and presenting yourself in a way that leaves nothing hidden is conforming to the world's view and influence which depicts women are objects, and their value is found in their exterior components. Now, do not get me wrong, I do not blame women for a man's inability to control his body and mind. I do believe that both women and men have bought into the influence of current worldly views and in turn have degraded and not valued their God-created bodies, souls, and spirits. Sex is a gift from God designed for the covenant relationship of marriage. Sex outside of that covenant relationship of marriage in any form is a poor substitute and will cause damage that only God can heal.

~

The entitlement and self-focused nature that is fed to those using pornography slowly brews and deeply wounds relationships. Pornography addiction is a symptom of something deeper that may be brought on by childhood traumas, abuse, or even generational curses, but the core of it is pride. That pride presents as entitlement. Pride and entitlement bring a sense of false superiority, and therefore denial about the state of depravity. Pornography is destructive and will take most further than they ever intended to go. The pride and entitlement mentality will grow as the addiction grows, and with it, other things will manifest including anger and control. How it manifests can be different I am sure, but from my experience, it became demonstrative and was erratic. It was unpredictable to the point of never knowing what the person could do; the outbursts that began and continued were like nothing I could have imagined. I tried to make excuses, reason it away, and blame it on physical conditions, but I was in denial for a long time.

I believe I was manipulated for a long time. Whether the manipulation was intentional or just a way to cover for the continued sin is debatable. When my former husband was manipulating me and trying to get me to believe I was the "crazy" one in order to protect his unfaithful behaviors, that was abusive. Being called "crazy" and having the facts and evidence of the sin choices manipulated was extremely damaging to my gut instincts and ability to make good decisions. Lying to a relationship partner causes damage, but it is also abusive deflecting, gaslighting, withholding truths, telling partial truths, and even blaming victims for their behaviors.

If your spouse is having a secret sexual life, it will divert their attention from the marital relationship as well as the family. When a spouse chooses to commit infidelity—whether by using pornography or with another person—families suffer. The minute someone has a deceptive, compartmentalized sex life, they must tell all sorts of lies and therefore are dishonest in their relationships with their spouse and family. This can be blatant lying or lying by omission or even partial lying. The manipulation and gaslighting (to gaslight is an act of undermining another person's reality by denying facts or invalidating their feelings) by the unfaithful spouse can damage the betrayed spouse's instincts, which is a survival instinct. If there have been many years full of lying and maintaining a secret life while pretending to be honest in a relationship or with family, this is damaging.

Something I discovered on my journey to healing from all the damage is that I am not an isolated case, and with that being said, many have experienced what is known as betrayal trauma. Betrayal trauma is simply an event of betrayal of one's primary relationship that one considers extremely disturbing or damaging. Trauma is defined as an event that overwhelms the central nervous system, altering the way we process and recall memories. I was glad when I realized there was a term that described exactly what I was dealing with and what I was feeling, as I could not articulate the depth of the pain and the impact on every facet of my life. Hearing this term and gaining understanding gave me great help on my road to recovery and I thank God for this insight.

Betrayal trauma manifests when one's reality of their relationship has been destroyed. I realized that I believed my former husband was a certain person with the same Christian values we had both shared for many years, only to discover that was not the case and trust was broken. It caused me to not trust myself. I felt shame and guilt and even blamed myself for what I may have done or did not do. It caused me to question the authenticity of my entire marriage. How could the man I loved betray me so deeply? I experienced not only pain, but panic, terror, and a feeling of helplessness and hopelessness. I had physical symptoms of high blood pressure, stomach issues, loss of sleep, as well as a thought life that wavered between trusting God and being mad at God. I viewed my physical appearance as not good enough, not sexy enough, not thin enough, not voluptuous enough ... not anything enough. Through my healing journey, I rediscovered I am enough and more than enough, as I am a daughter of God!

> Your light will break forth like the dawn, and your healing will quickly appear.
> – Isaiah 58:8 NIV

Chapter 16

It is in Christ that we find out who we are and what we are living for. Long before we first heard of Christ and got our hopes up, he had his eye on us, had designs on us for glorious living, part of the overall purpose he is working out everything and everyone.

Ephesians 1:11-12 MSG

SPRING BEGAN TO APPEAR BEFORE I knew it. There were a couple court hearings which seemed to be groundhog day all over again. The same items and issues were addressed. It was agreed through meetings in the offices of my attorney and his attorney that I would get the contents of the marital home with the exception of some specific items he requested. I honestly wanted nothing but the photos of my children, my mother's china, and my grandmother's silver. I had come to a place of acceptance, but grieving is still a process, and I would find myself experiencing those stages of grief when I least expected them. In the midst of it all, I had peace. I was determined to go on with my life and I would trust God. I knew I was going to be alright.

Near the final months, I stopped going to my counselor after returning to see her for a short time. She was an amazing help and comfort during this long season, but I knew I was going to be O.K. Besides, I was no longer covered by my former husband's insurance. My counselor had extended much grace regarding payment, and I knew God used her for that season and now it was over. I would recommend her to anyone going through brokenness, grief, or any other emotional or mental difficulty. Counseling is a tremendous help, and too often those who are Spirit-filled believers do not recommend it or think you are not spiritual enough if you seek counseling. I disagree with that viewpoint, as I believe God gives gifts to the body of Christ, and that includes people with wisdom from God who can help guide, comfort, and be a voice of reason in order for full healing to take place.

I learned and accepted that I had a part to play in the unhealthy cycle I had been in for nearly four years. I so wanted reconciliation and restoration that I oftentimes took matters into my own hands, thinking if I gave myself to my former husband more or ignored the behaviors and loved him more, it would somehow bring about his change of heart. I wanted to jump right to reconciliation and trust again without true repentance, consistent accountability, and without consequences for the sin choices he made. We must go through the difficulty of true repentance, be willing to be accountable, and deal with the consequences of our choices (which will in turn promote healing and forgiveness) in order to have the reconciliation and restoration that God orchestrates. I believe any person can be restored and renewed in their mind, but repentance must happen first. True repentance happens when we own our poor choices, we no longer lie and cover, and there is consistent evidence of that change. Consistency is key, and this happens for longer than a few days or weeks. Rebuilding trust takes time, so in order to have full restoration and be reconciled, there must be rebuilt trust. I believe both the husband and wife must be willing to do whatever it takes to restore a marriage, including being transparent, understanding that damage was done, and then accepting the truth that the relationship needs to heal, and healing takes time.

My hope is that my fellow brothers and sisters in Christ would acknowledge the need for true repentance when it comes to the pornography epidemic. I can remember reaching out to a pastor who I thought my former husband would talk to after he refused to speak to our overseer. When I called that pastor early on in our separation because my former husband was demonstrating such chaotic behavior (like throwing trash onto the front yard of the marital home, including old appliances from rentals and debris from construction sites) and pleaded with him to call my husband, to reach out to him, I was accused of "lying on the man of God." I was told, "You should not be saying these things about your husband." When I shared that he was continuing to view pornography and had pictures of other women on his phone I was told, "You are not a good wife. You have a Jezebel spirit." I sent this pastor pictures of the front yard and told him that I was not making this up.

He refuted my claims and said, "You should be ashamed of yourself for calling me." I realized that there were not many who would or could reach out to my husband, nor anyone he would listen to. As I look back, I realize that part of the problem was that my former husband had no accountability to anyone and there was no one to pull him out of the fire. His associates fueled the fire. They laughed at his pictures, they ridiculed his wife, they looked at dating sites together, and they encouraged the single life even while knowing he was married.

A woman is told, "You are to stay in your marriage even if there is infidelity, verbal, or emotional abuse," and some even rationalize physical abuse. Women then bear the burden that if they leave, they betray God, and we all know "God hates divorce." Somehow it does not matter if the husband broke vows, continues in infidelities and betrayal—the wife is to stay. The women are told they are responsible for breaking the covenant by leaving, but in actuality, it was the husband who broke the covenant the first time he chose to participate in infidelity. In the church world, there seems to be no accountability for the one who broke the vows. The wife is blamed for the husband looking at pornography because she is "not doing enough to fulfill her husband's needs," or it has been said to some women, "You let yourself go." Let me be clear in saying that when a man or woman makes a choice to sin, they are the only ones held accountable for their choice. We will all stand before God and give account for our actions and responses. I would encourage every man and woman to respond to any circumstance according to scripture and allow your life to be a living example of Jesus in our actions and deeds.

Our final court date was set, and it was agreed that I would move into one of the rentals. I was permitted to begin working on renovating the home before the final court date. During that time, I changed the locks on the home and brought over a chair and a small table so I could sit, make my lists for materials, and drink my coffee. One day when I was pulling into the driveway, a vehicle was pulling out that I did not recognize. I followed the vehicle and discovered it was my former husband. I went back to the house and discovered that the back door was missing its new lock and my chair, table, and the fireplace cover were gone. I had to notify my attorney and my former husband was forced to return the items. I had to have new locks put on the door once again. Eventually, a whole new door was installed that prevented anyone from breaking in.

As I began working on my new home and packing the things from the marital home a few months before the final hearing, I began to know I was coming through this season. I still grieved the great loss, but I had a renewed sense of hope. I knew God had walked me through and carried me at times during this most difficult season in my life. I had hope that my future would be bright. I was content with being in my new home with my youngest son and my college-aged son when he was home for break, and I would enjoy being YiaYia ("grandma" in Greek) to my grandchildren. I had promised the Lord from the beginning that no matter what, I would serve Him. I made plans to go on more mission trips as soon as I was able, and God opened the doors, and I would continue to speak of all His wondrous works. I continued my radio program every Friday during these difficult three and half years, and I continued in the ministry. It was only God who gave me strength and enabled me to persevere through adversity.

Two weeks before the final court date I learned that my father had died. My father and I were not close, but it seemed the timing could not have been worse and yet it provided closure. I assumed the funeral would be well before the final court date, but it was not. The funeral service was planned for nearly two weeks later which meant I would be heading to Cleveland for my father's funeral three days before the final court date. The last time I had seen my father was over two years prior, and he had been in the ICU. I had gone to the hospital with one of my sons, and I was able to tell my father that I loved him, I forgave him, and I was O.K. I shared with him that I had a good life and that God had blessed me with a family. I was able to pray with him and tell him God knows his heart (he was unable to speak) and all he has to do is speak to God in his heart and accept Jesus as Savior and ask for forgiveness. The Lord told me that would be the last time I saw him, but I did not know it would be over two years before he died and that he actually got out of ICU and went to my sister's home.

I went to the funeral on Friday evening for the viewing. There, I met two brothers and two sisters face-to-face for the first time. I had already met one of my sisters a few years prior and remained in contact through social media. She had a close relationship with our father and took care of all the details for the funeral. I got a hotel room for the night in order to attend the funeral the next day. Two of my sons would be coming in the morning. My father was an over forty-year member of Hell's Angels. I had never experienced a viewing and funeral where so many came from all over the United States to pay their respects to a "brother." Two of my sons attended the actual funeral with me on Saturday and met my extended family (who were new to me too). Hundreds of motorcycles followed the hearse to the graveyard in a parade. The casket was lowered into the hole and two dump truck loads of dirt were then delivered next to the hole. Many "brothers" took turns shoveling the dirt and covering the casket of my father. This continued until it was fully covered and tamped down. I had never experienced anything like that, nor had my sons who came. It was a beautiful picture of brotherhood and something the church world could take a lesson from. The love and camaraderie shown were exceptional. I do wish I had the opportunity to say a few words, as there was a captive audience, but it was not given. I believed the encounters I had with individuals would point to Jesus. My two sons and I attended the lunch afterward at the local chapter clubhouse and we were treated exceptionally well, as many knew I was his oldest daughter. The food was a great surprise. I was expecting a cookout, but was treated to a chef-prepared, plated meal that was amazing and delicious. I am so thankful to have had the privilege to attend, have closure, and experience the whole event. Look, there are not too many people who get to go to the local Hell's Angels clubhouse and have a five-star lunch. What I originally thought was bad timing ended up giving me hope and peace. I returned home knowing that in two days, the final court date would be here.

Chapter 17

He heals the wounds of every shattered heart.
– Psalm 147 TPT

Now may God, the fountain of hope, fill you to overflowing with uncontainable joy and perfect peace as you trust in him. And may the power of the Holy Spirit continually surround your life with his super-abundance until you radiate with hope!
– Romans 15:13 TPT

THE DAY ARRIVED AND I had no idea what to wear. What do you wear to the event that will end your thirty-six-year marriage? I remember I settled for black pants and a white blouse. It all seemed surreal. Today would begin "the hearing" and I had to arrive early to meet with my attorney so he could tell me how the hearing would proceed. We sat in a conference room and he shared his binder with me. There would be questions under oath, and all would be rehashed. It was overwhelming to think of all the people who would hear the ugly tale, and it would all be recorded. My attorney advised me to remain calm and try not to get too emotional. There was a knock on the door and my attorney was asked to come out in the hallway. He came back in to tell me the judge had called both attorneys into his chambers. It felt like hours as I sat there waiting. When my attorney returned, he informed me there would be no hearing and that the judge demanded both parties come to an agreement today—that this had gone on long enough. I was relieved to hear that, and I also felt it was God's grace that it did not have to happen. The attorneys then began negotiation. The final agreed-upon terms were those things we had originally requested. On paper, it would appear my former husband received the majority of the marital assets and that he won. I had peace with the terms and there is no price you can put on peace. The final typing out and correcting of details seemed endless. I was left in the conference room alone.

The court clerk came in to check on me because I was emotional. She got me tissues and said, "This has been a long case and you have been through a lot. I know you will get through this and will be alright." At first I did not understand why I was so emotional. I had known for months that it was really over. I had come to the place of acceptance. I was moving on with my life. I realized that day that grief does not really end. It may manifest in diverse ways at different times. I had come to a place of acceptance and had regained hope for my future without my former husband, but that did not mean the loss would ever disappear. I learned how you can grieve the loss and still go forward and find happiness and live an abundant life full of hope and expectancy. I believe it is only because of Jesus that this is possible.

Things had taken a different turn than I had expected or believed for when we first separated. I fought for my marriage and believed for full restoration, but at the beginning of the year I came to the place of accepting reality once I was countered for divorce. While I had biblical justification to end my marriage, I chose to fight for it. The truth is that I could not fight alone and sometimes restoration does not happen. I had hoped for our happy ending, that our story would be full restoration, but it was not. Accepting my future that looks nothing like what I so desperately wanted, prayed for, and stood in faith for is not easy, and yet I have a peace from God that surpasses all my understanding. I know one thing: forgiveness always works for good. I chose and will continue to choose forgiveness.

I knew God had walked me through the whole season. I knew in my heart I had chosen forgiveness, and I knew I was going on with the Lord. I am so grateful that God's healing power has touched my heart. I knew I had cried buckets of tears that did not go unnoticed by God, and I knew through forgiveness I had no bitterness or resentment. Knowing all of that did not change the grief of the loss and the finality of it all. We had to go back into the courtroom to go through the procedures. I was asked my name and then I was asked if I understood I was being granted a divorce that I filed for. I answered and said, "I never filed for divorce, I filed for separation."

The judge looked down at his papers, corrected his question, and said, "You understand you are being countered with divorce on your filing of separation and that today you will be legally divorced?"

I had to answer, "Yes," so it could all be recorded. The tears just escaped my eyes as much as I tried to not release them in that courtroom. I replied, "Yes," to the judge. The same question was asked to my former husband, and he also answered, "Yes." The judge declared that we were officially divorced. After four hours or more in the conference room, and going back and forth with attorneys that day, it took less than twenty minutes in the courtroom to finalize the end of the marriage. My former husband immediately left, and I sat in the chair trying to compose myself. My attorney walked out with me, and my former husband's attorney was behind us. They began talking about sending documents and such. I got on the elevator and walked to my car. It was over.

I had my close friends praying for me that day and they checked on me throughout the day. I texted them to let them know it was over and headed home. My youngest son was in the kitchen when I returned. He knew what the day was and could see I had been emotional. I hugged him and told him court was over and I was going to go lay down for a little bit. He was headed to work. I remember laying on my bed experiencing such deep grief, but I also remember feeling relieved that it was finally over. There was closure. I had a presence of peace in my room. I knew God was holding me. There would be no more attorneys, no more meetings, no more arguing over possessions, money, or "things." I was also relieved that I would not have to deal with the lies and continued choice to view porn. I was tired of competing for so long with images in my own mind of what was viewed. I was tired from trying to be a good Christian wife and pray it away. I was tired from feeling the shame of a failed marriage. I was tired of not feeling good enough for my former spouse. I was tired of the rumors. I was tired of trying to protect all my children. I was tired of feeling like I let God down. So, I slept until late evening.

I woke up and ate a little something and went back to bed after my son got home. The next morning, I went to what was to be my new house in 120 days. I had 120 days to finish renovating and move. There was a lot of work ahead, but I was determined to get it done. Honestly, it became invigorating to work on my new home. I hired contractors, made my own plans for what I wanted to be done, and did a lot of work myself. I had always had my own tools and had learned a lot over the years from all the renovations I had played a part in previously. This time I would be able to do it the way I wanted with detail. I would be downsizing, to say the least, so many of the things I once owned would be sold. I made plans to have a major sale and I would be furnishing my new home with fresh things. It was my new beginning, and I knew I had come through to the other side.

There was a lot of praise at the new house as I worked. I had the opportunity to pray with and for some of the workers and contractors. As my home began to come back to life, it was a great representation of God's gift of new beginnings to me. He walked me through the toughest season of my life, and I know there were times he carried me. I never imagined my marriage coming to an end, but I know God never left me nor forsook me. His presence was real to me at a level I had never before experienced, even at my lowest points. His grace was more tangible than I had ever known, and His love was greater than I ever imagined.

I finished the house. I sold a lot of material things at my tag sale. I moved by the given deadline with the help of all my children and their spouses. I decorated, assembled some furniture, had furniture delivered, and enjoyed the peace and new surroundings. Things had changed and my life would never be the same and I had hope.

I would like to say everything between my former husband, and I became peaceful, but unfortunately it did not. I had to permanently block his number as I began receiving voicemails and texts right after our final hearing. I would get things left on my porch, he would drive by yelling out the window, and leave countless letters in the mailbox that were unkind. I had to install cameras and the police were called numerous times. To be honest, I was afraid at times, and it was difficult living in the same town. I had to change my running schedule daily so I felt safe and that I was not being stalked. Police said there was nothing they could do about any of it since there were no "blatant threats." It was humiliating to get mail that the mailman delivered, and the envelope had terrible words on it referring to me. I even had to deal with my four-by-eight-foot Christian signs that I had in front of the marital home—which was on a major highway—for many years being removed and replaced with a horrendous word being spray-painted on the base that referred to me so many could see (fortunately, it soon came down and he put back up the Christian signs). So often, I wanted to scream, "I was never unfaithful! I have never even seen another man naked, whether on video or picture, in thirty-six years." Yet I knew there was no defending myself and God knew all. I rested in God's comfort and peace. One of the letters I received in the mail was a letter I had written to my former husband in the beginning of the year that he sent back to me. I knew when I wrote this letter it was closure and I had embraced true forgiveness. The following are a few excerpts from that letter:

Dear ----,

36 years ago, on a Friday night we walked into a church together ... We were baptized and gave our life to Jesus. Who knew 2 years after we met that is where we would be on a Friday night? ... I was sixteen you were twenty-one when we met ...2 weeks after our salvation we were married.

... we became a family of 8. 1 daughter and 5 sons with 6 grandchildren and more on the way. God has been more than good to us. He has blessed us with children, grandchildren and provided always. You have always worked hard. I shall never forget how God saved us. I am so grateful and thankful and can never praise Him enough for blessing me to be a wife, have children and now grandchildren.

I share in these few pages just a glimpse of our life ... I choose to remember our life this way. I do not know how or why things have come this far from where we began. Yes, I could list some obvious things but ... I will choose to remember this part of our life together ...

I cannot change you, force you to choose me or even make you understand. If I knew the pain that would be experienced 30+ years later, I would still choose to be ... the mother of your children ... you have had a lifetime of my love and I will never forget that.

My love always, Theresa

I knew I was free of bitterness and unforgiveness. I had no malice toward my former husband. I prayed for him to be restored to right relationship with his Savior, as that was more important than our marriage ever being restored. I continued to pray for my children and that their father would desire to restore relationship with them and be the father they so desperately need. I had newfound peace, and it was priceless. I had a new sense of peace since the beginning of the year. After three and a half years, although the loss was grievous beyond words, I was going on with the Lord and felt hope. My future looked bright, and I never imagined what would be ahead. I never expected just how God would restore me and allow me to experience love again. You see, for years I had become a super detective because I knew something was not right. I had walked on eggshells for countless years, always felt small, had anger, and was hypervigilant (constantly aware of my surroundings, picking up on little things that were off). I was alone and yet married for many years. I had sought out and discovered that in fact, I was not crazy, and all the things I felt the Holy Spirit was showing me were true and all the hidden things had been exposed. Unfortunately, the final outcome was not what I expected or wanted. Reconciliation did not happen. Restoration did not happen. True repentance with the fruits thereof did not happen—but that is not to say it cannot happen in the future for the father of my children. I continue to pray for my former husband because I know God's hand reaches far and desires his sons and daughters to come home. I learned that forgiveness is not the absence of pain, but it is a daily choice I had to make and continue to make. Forgiveness is saturated in God's grace and mercy and that is why I will always pray for spiritual restoration for anyone who has fallen away from Jesus. I know I had to go through the grief process and come to a place of acceptance in order to walk completely in forgiveness and receive God's given hope for my future, and I did it. There were no shortcuts. I had to feel every pain and deal with my emotions that manifested in anger, depression, and hopelessness. I was able to feel the presence of God in the midst of it because of the Holy Spirit that lives in me. I learned to walk in the fact and not just recite the scripture that in my weakness (pain, frailties, imperfections), He is made strong in me. I had come to a place of full surrender and allowed Him to heal my broken heart and fully mend and bind all my wounds, so it was no longer apparent on the outside.

God had begun healing the million pieces of my broken heart from the beginning, and He reconstructed the brokenness and infused joy into what I thought was permanently damaged. He took a million little pieces and fully restored function in every area of my life. All the work God did on the inside has manifested on the outside and prayerfully reflects His love, His care, His joy, and His faithfulness to me for the rest of the world to see.

> He heals the brokenhearted and binds up their wounds.
> – Psalm 147:3 NIV

Also from Theresa Marie:

For contact or scheduling:
Theresa Marie Ministries
P.O. Box 923
Marion, OH 43302

Email: theresamarieministries@gmail.com

Facebook: www.facebook.com/theresamarieministries